Colonial Bureaucracy
and Creating Underdevelopment:
Tanganyika, 1919–1940

Colonial Bureaucracy
and Creating Underdevelopment:
Tanganyika, 1919–1940

D. M. P. M c C A R T H Y

The Iowa State University Press

A M E S

© 1982 The Iowa State University Press. All rights reserved

Composed and printed by The Iowa State University Press, Ames, Iowa 50010

First edition, 1982

Library of Congress Cataloging in Publication Data

McCarthy, Dennis Michael Patrick, 1944–
  Colonial bureaucracy and creating underdevelopment.

  Bibliography: p.
  Includes index.
  1. Tanzania—Economic policy. 2. Tanzania—Colonial influence—History. 3. Great Britain—Colonies—Africa—Administration—History. 4. Bureaucracy—Tanzania—History. I. Title.
  HC885.M32   338.9678   80-28269
  ISBN 0-8138-1590-8

TO THE UNITED REPUBLIC OF TANZANIA

. . . forsan et haec olim meminisse juvabit.

—Virgil *Aeneid* 1.203.

CONTENTS

PREFACE

T W O of the most cutting problems of our times are the related concerns of this book: underdevelopment and government bureaucracy. The history of each, particularly in an African context, has so far been studied largely in isolation from the other. When scholars have occasionally and casually intersected the two histories, the actions of colonial bureaucracies, which are the direct ancestors of most legally independent African governments, appear as adjuncts to the processes deemed central by most persons discussing the causes and cures for underdevelopment in the "Third World."

Preoccupied with the search for a "new international economic order" as the major solution to a host of specific problems superficially aggregated as underdevelopment, many are inclined to view the past primarily as the emergence of "old international economic orders" of various sorts. In fact, the leitmotif of much current writing on the origins and entrenchment of underdevelopment is the evolution of a hydra-headed entity called variously the European world-economy, European world-system, capitalist world-system, or world-economy.

The most influential version of this process is a story of external exploitation and conflict told in categories highly aggregative for both economies and people. To oversimplify, many locate the roots of underdevelopment in the manipulation of internal or "indigenous" economies and their respective elements by agents of "external interests," who are usually the impresarios of overseas economies of varying magnitudes. And the human actors in this drama are themselves collectivized. Rarely do human beings appear in current scholarship as individuals with personal perceptions of their own goals. It is conflict between or among the groups and classes to which scholars have retrospectively assigned people that resounds in works highlighting the exploitation of labor and other resources associated with Africa's alleged incorporation into the "world-economy."

While the history of underdevelopment is marked by more than an esthetic imbalance between cosmic themes and limited methods, the history of African government bureaucracy during the colonial period is characterized by narrow rubrics and heavy reliance on published evidence. Most studies that touch on some aspect of colonial bureaucracy take one or more of the following approaches.

The first is to write almost self-contained administrative history, which all too often has multiplied antiseptic descriptions of such external features as the size of the bureaucratic establishment and the number of ordinances promulgated on particular subjects. This genre of administrative history sometimes includes fascinating human interest material on specific personalities. The net effect of writing ponderously about structures and crisply about people, and often in that process artificially separating the two, is to divert attention from the crucial impact of both on their environments.

A second approach appears in some works more imperial than colonial in focus. It is most concerned with the diplomacy and politics of how which European countries came to control what portions of Africa during the "scramble for Africa" in the late nineteenth century. The history of colonial administration is here treated almost wholly as the result of those "higher level" imperial forces, never as the source of specific phenomena that require analysis on a case-by-case basis.

A third method, analytically akin in some ways to the second, is to regard "colonial economic policy" only as a transformation or further elaboration of some country's "imperial economic policy." That is, what happened in a particular overseas possession of a European country in matters economic can best be explained with reference mainly to the needs of that European country and/or its empire. The third approach takes for granted the logical stability of the category, "colonial economic policy."

This third approach dominates the current research that does intersect the histories of underdevelopment and African colonial bureaucracy. The rubric "colonial economic policy" might overemphasize similar though not always identical elements in the approaches of various on-the-spot colonial bureaucracies and blur or even erase significant variation. For the moment the construct has great utility as a set of prefabricated building blocks for those who fashion spatially aggregative economic systems, whether of the continental, imperial, or global varieties. It is ironic that scholars who have recognized the complexity and diversity of Africa in most every other way should treat the concepts of bureaucracy and economy so homogeneously. It is bewildering that some of the scholars who rightly criticized the older genres of imperial history as neglecting the complicated nature of "African initiatives and responses" during the period of European rule should be making similar errors of compression concerning bureaucracy and economy during the colonial period.

Perhaps the most fundamental conviction, though not stated so bluntly, is that if you have seen one colonial bureaucracy in action, you have seen them all. But we have not yet witnessed even one colonial administration really "in action." Here the problems of evidence and method become crucial. The written evidence employed to date has included then contemporaneous published documents. When unpublished material has been used, it is usually of the sort found in various public and private European archives. The internal records of particular colonial bureaucracies, located in African archives, remain insufficiently analyzed. There is no comprehensive inside story of any African colonial bureaucracy based on a probing examination of its own records in conjunction with those aforementioned sources. Nor are there any studies that systematically explore the relationships between colonial bureaucracy and underdevelopment. It seems appropriate, therefore, to present the first such inside story that begins to relate the histories of underdevelopment and African government bureaucracy in the deliberate manner both these important phenomena require.

Why and how I have studied inter-war Tanganyika is in lesser part an historical accident, in greater part an endeavor to present part of the past of a country that is in the forefront of a slowly emerging Western appreciation of Africa. I began as a second-year Yale graduate student in 1968, when I took a writing seminar which William Roger Louis had dedicated to Tanzania before 1940. He emphasized the inter-war period, because the fifty-year waiting rule, governing access to certain confidential documents in British public metropolitan archives, had recently been reduced to thirty years, and if we discovered a topic during the seminar for a doctoral dissertation, we might be among the first to mine that declassified material in later research. How prescient he was. I so discovered and so researched. Leonard Thompson became my supervisor in 1969; under his guidance I prepared a 1972 dissertation on the inter-war Tanganyika bureaucracy, which is the crude and sometimes remote antecedent of the present work.

I did not visit Tanzania until 1973. I applied for research clearance to the National Archives in late 1969, was rejected in August 1970, tried again and again, and finally got it in 1972. I could not go then. Economic necessity, and the Yale Graduate School's program-completion rule, dictated the production of a dissertation. I had no money to make the trip in

1972 and was looking for a job. I found one but feared my goal of researching in Tanzania would slip away under the pressures of first-year teaching and the difficulties of getting money as now junior faculty with nothing in print. Louis G. Geiger, my first chairman at Iowa State University, urged me when I arrived in 1972 to apply for a Social Science Research Council grant. I was awarded this money and went to Dar es Salaam in June 1973. Without Professor Geiger's gentle but forceful prodding and the SSRC's financial vote of confidence, this monograph could not have been written. In Dar es Salaam I studied, among other documents, the Secretariat files, which contain valuable evidence illuminating the internal workings of the Tanganyika administration.

Getting research clearance for the National Archives in Dar es Salaam was itself a major lesson in bureaucracy. I shall not provide here every detail of that thirty-month quest, although the subject may rate attention in any future memoir I might write. Now I want to thank in the strongest possible terms Kenneth Kirkwood, the Rhodes Professor of Race Relations in Oxford University, for his indispensable diplomatic good offices. As I have written various drafts of the "final version" of this book over the last five years, I received significant assistance of one type or another from Ralph Austen, Fred Carstensen, Hamilton Cravens, Thomas Kompas, Richard Lowitt, Harry Miskimin, William Parker, Leonard Thompson, J. Mills Thornton, III, and Rick Wolff. Three people deserve special mention. Although Professor Thompson inherited direction of my graduate school work (no doubt one of the more curious legacies he faced), he has always treated me with exceptional grace and provided unfailing encouragement. If there is any one individual who is responsible for my emergence as an economic historian, that person is Professor Miskimin, whose own exquisite sense of understatement is why I say nothing more about him. The scholar most immediately responsible for the publication of this book is Fred Carstensen, who has never let our longstanding friendship dilute in any way his criticism of my work.

Numerous people have facilitated other aspects of this long search. The staffs of the Public Record Office, London, and the National Archives, Dar es Salaam, along with those of the Rhodes House, Boston University, and Yale University libraries, taught me much about the mechanics of research. Everyone connected with St. Antony's College, Oxford, created one of the most stimulating intellectual environments I have ever experienced. On the home front, I cannot adequately thank Ms. Susan E. Ulrickson, Ms. Tamara Huber, and Ms. Laura Helmers for typing portions of the manuscript. Nor can I sufficiently recognize Ms. Carole Kennedy for her efforts in coordinating its preparation.

I also wish to thank the editor and publisher of *The International Journal of African Historical Studies* for permission to reprint portions of an earlier article of mine, "Organizing Underdevelopment from the Inside: The Bureaucratic Economy in Tanganyika, 1919–1940," 10(1977), pp. 573–99. In at times modified fashion, chapter 1 incorporates pp. 577–83; chapter 2, p. 585, pp. 587–91; chapter 5, parts of pp. 585–87; chapter 6, pp. 591–98, excepting a fragment from pp. 594–95, which is used in chapter 7.

D.M.P.M.

Colonial Bureaucracy
and Creating Underdevelopment:
Tanganyika, 1919–1940

UGANDA
PROTECTORATE
LAKE VICTORIA
KENYA   COLONY
NAIROBI

BUKOBA
MUSOMA
KAJIADO

Ukerewe Is.
MWANZA
MASWA
LAKE
NATRON

BIHARAMULO
Serengeti
Plains
LAKE
EYASI
ARUSHA
Mt. Meru
X 4553
Mt. Kilimanjaro
5890
VOI
MOSHI

BELGIAN
CONGO
KIBONDO
KAHAMA
Manjonwa R. Sibiti
R. MBULU
MKALAMA
KINYANGIRI
SAME
MOMBASA

NZEGA
LUSHOTO
KOROGWE

KASULU
Malagarazi R.
SINGIDA
KONDOA
HANDENI
TANGA
PANGANI
Pemba Is.

LAKE TANGANYIKA
Ugalla R.
TABORA
MANYONI
DODOMA
MPWAPWA
BAGAMOYO
Zanzibar Is.

KITUNDA
Njombe R.
Great
Ruaha R.
MOROGORO
KILOSA
DAR ES SALAAM

SUMBAWANGA
LAKE
RUKWA
IRINGA
Ndembera R.
Little Ruaha
Kilombero R.
Rufiji R.
UTETE
Mafia Is.
INDIAN
OCEAN

MBEYA
TUKUYU
NJOMBE
MAHENGE
Morongondu R.
KILWA

RHODESIA
NYASALAND
LAKE NYASA
LIWALE
LINDI
MIKINDANI

MASASI
NEWALA

SONGEA
TUNDURU
River
Rovuma

PORTUGUESE EAST AFRICA

RAILROADS ┼┼┼┼
ROADS ────

0   100   200
Scale in miles

1

Introducing the Bureaucratic Economy: The ABCs of Organization

THE original root meaning of the word "Tanganyika" challenges explorers of all genres to probe beyond this East African territory's Indian Ocean coastline. Tanganyika means literally the "bush behind Tanga." These roots suggest a dichotomy of both geography and knowledge. Tanga, a port on the northeastern coast of the country, is the one specific place in the territory's name. The rest of the title is vague, referring to the bush behind the town. The geographical division between coast and interior suggested by "Tanganyika" is matched by differences in knowledge about activities on the coast and in the interior. At least until the middle of the nineteenth century, the interior of Tanganyika remained less well known to outsiders than its Indian Ocean coast. About this time there began thrusts inland of the peoples that give Tanzania (as the linking in nomenclature of *Tan*ganyika and *Zan*zibar has been known from 1964) an historical legacy of foreign impact with such complicated skeins. The penetrators included different kinds of Arab and Asiatic business people, as well as nationals from several European countries, especially Germany and England. Each *mzungu* (Kiswahili for European or, more generally, white person) was pursuing some activity or activities—exploring, trading, soldiering, farming, catechizing, and administering—in ways that often mixed personal and patriotic objectives.

The land has as its principal topographical feature thousands of square miles of plains. These are found at varying altitudes, from a few hundred feet above sea level near the coast to heights of 6,000 feet in the north (the Serengeti Plains), in the Southern Highlands, and in Ufipa in the west. The central plateau is defined along its eastern and western margins by escarpments, which fall on the west to the level of Lakes Tanganyika and Nyasa. The northern region contains the major mountains of the country, Kilimanjaro and Meru. About three-fourths of the territory has a mean annual temperature variation from sixty-nine to eighty-one degrees Fahrenheit; the minimum range is from forty-six to sixty-six degrees.

The antecedent peoples, some of whose ancestors migrated to East Africa from elsewhere on the continent, are too often perceived only in categories that permit little room for differentiation. During two periods of formal colonial rule, under Germany from 1888–1918 and England from 1919–1961, their most common appellation, in the colloquial vocabulary of cultural imperialism and condescension, was "the natives." Those who aimed at greater sophistication would designate particular "natives" as members of some ethnically distinct "tribe," sometimes when prior group cohesiveness did not warrant such a label.

A nascent sense of complexity for social and political customs slowly emerged in those who ruled and researched them. But the "indigenous administered" ("the Africans" or "the blacks"), as distinguished from the "non-indigenous administered" (Arabs, Asiatic Indians, and some *wazungu*), would rarely be portrayed in terms any less gross than those that still dominate the jejune vocabulary of much contemporary economic and some anthropological literature for describing "indigenous economic activity." In 1934, for example, most British administrators posited eighty-eight "tribes" within Tanganyika. Thirty-six were publicly classified as agricultural, pastoral, or a combination of the two. Only the Masai and Tusi were completely pastoral. Fourteen were depicted as completely agricultural—Luguru, Mwera, Zigua, Ngindo, Zaramo, Zinza, Yao, Hamba, Nyamwezi, Nyasa, Nyaihangiro, Rufiji, Makonde, and Sumbwa. Twenty supposedly followed mixed agricultural and pastoral practices—Chagga, Mbulu, Kuria, Nyakyusa, Nyaturu, Sukuma, Jita, Fipa, Kukwe, Shambaa, Pare, Ngoni, Kerewe, Sandawe, Hehe, Gogo, Irangi, Iramba, Bena, and Ha.[1]

Tanganyika Territory encompassed most of what had been German East Africa. Great Britain administered it as a League of Nations mandate after Germany's defeat in World War I. It generally did not offer an environment conducive to the development of sustained economic activity. At least two-thirds of the country was closed to cultivation during the inter-war period because of the tsetse fly and lack of water. Only ten percent of the territory was then well watered, and this area contained about two-thirds of the total population. Most of the arable land was in the northern and southern highlands, along the coast, and in the western lake region. The geographical center of the country did not receive adequate rainfall and, without irrigation, could not reliably support sustained agriculture. Most enduring economic activity concentrated about the territory's periphery.

From 1919 a British colonial administration headquartered in Dar es Salaam was overseer of this territory. This institution did exhibit the ethos inherent in the British overseas colonial service. Many of its members preached and practiced their own versions of "hard work," "pulling one's weight in the boat," and "fair play."[2] But the administration was not a simple conduit for policies originating elsewhere in the imperial organization. Nor was it a servant obedient to the demands of various private external interests or an enforcer of the wishes of alien groups within the territory. In fact, its agents strove to organize Tanganyika according to their own requirements for stability. These modes of organization reinforced some broad imperial objectives, and there were occasional communities of interest between the Tanganyika bureaucracy and private groups both inside and outside the territory. There were also arguments inside the administration and some variation in on-the-spot implementation of directives from Dar es Salaam. Yet from action as well as inaction came an administrative pattern of behavior designed to service a bureaucratic economy above all others.

This was an economy in the most basic sense: an organization of the forms, contents, and locations of production, distribution, and exchange in ways that supplied the revenue and order the bureaucracy demanded. This economy functioned in ways that conflicted with what some agents representing other economic interests wanted. The economy gained its coherence from extraction and control, sometimes joined together under the rubric of regulation. This economy imposed on Tanganyikans a series of extractions, distortions, and dislocations that can be analyzed as internally generated forms of underdevelopment.

This book examines all those aspects of the bureaucratic economy in detail. The next two sections deal with some basic facts about the organization of the Tanganyika bureaucracy and its economy. The first discusses the general problem of stability in relation to internal administration structures and their extensions. The second focuses on the bureaucratic economy—its axioms of organization and calculus of maximization and minimization.

THE BUREAUCRACY AND STABILITY

During the inter-war period Tanganyika's administrators professed several general goals for their territory and its residents. Article 3 of the British Mandate for East Africa made this administration responsible for the "peace, order and good government of the territory" and urged it to "promote to the utmost the material and moral well-being and the social progress" of the area's inhabitants.[3] At that time few questioned the legitimacy of those objectives, but some questioned priorities. Donald Cameron, who governed Tanganyika from 1925 through 1931, addressed the language of the mandate and admitted, "It has always occurred to me as a very strange thing that the material well-being was put before the moral well-being. In Tanganyika . . . we are putting the moral and social progress first, the material well-being to follow afterwards. There is no reason why it should not follow just a few steps behind."[4]

Whatever ranking of these ill-defined versions of progress they preferred, most bureaucrats considered how their daily actions were affected by a central administrative canon: the efficient preservation of stability within the territory. One should, therefore, examine what stability meant to this institution and its staff.

Most administrators construed it in at least two general senses. On the most superficial level, it meant an absence of physical threats to bureaucratic hegemony over the territory. In the end, the bureaucracy always had its police, backed by the King's African Rifles and the Royal Air Force. More basically, stability meant achieving the most desirable combinations of continuity and change over a range of situations. For the Tanganyika bureaucracy, those blends emphasized continuity but permitted, however slightly, elements of controlled change.

To define acceptable manifestations of these forces, then, became a key administrative problem. Most bureaucrats relied on fundamental conceptions of three related but distinct notions—standardization, unification, and integration. The influence of these perceptions on organization in every dimension was pervasive. It encompassed internal administrative structures, their extensions, and the bureaucratic economy itself. The following condensed table of organization concentrates on internal administrative structures and their extensions.

At first glance, the territorial table of organization would seem straightforward. The apex was the central bureaucracy in Dar es Salaam, which consisted of the Governor and the Secretariat. They were surrounded by the Legislative and Executive Councils, various specialized departments, and several advisory boards with mixed official and unofficial memberships. Farther down the chain of command were commissioners of the territory's provinces. Subordinate to them were the officers of the many districts. Under each specialized department were local technical officers, who were to cooperate with their respective district (administrative) officers. The district officers "advised" indigenous leaders of the local Native Authorities on a wide range of matters. These authorities were the most prominent extensions of internal administrative structures.

Standardization, perhaps the least ambiguous concept, had the most extensive applications. These appeared in the daily conduct of administration and in the design of general structures. Examples of daily administration are too numerous and tedious to mention here; one need only cite paperwork which, however voluminous its forms, expresses the homogenizing tendency of bureaucracy with special bluntness. As for general structures, one application of standardization of form deserves special mention: the spread of so-called Native Authorities throughout the territory.

In 1925 Tanganyikan administrators, led by Governor Cameron, began to articulate purposes and methods of "native administration" in the rhetoric of indirect rule. Indirect administration, which consisted of many local Native Authorities, miniaturized some structures of the central bureaucracy itself and thus seemed to promote a stability congenial to that parent institution. For example, each local authority had its own treasury and court. Staffs of those authorities were charged with performing duties corresponding in breadth to concerns of the center's specialized departments. Rarely was this a performance in depth. Native Authority budgets were always modest, and a significant portion of available money was spent on "administrative expenses."

The fact that Native Administration spent most on self-maintenance introduces the more difficult notions of unification and integration. The precise legal relationship between native administrations and parent bureaucracy was ambiguous. But the nature of the power connection rested, in part, on clear but narrow meanings of unification and integration. In one dimension, official unification was an endeavor to express anterior ethnic tradition and organization within a more standardized framework. This was a reorganization of localisms that altered appearance more than substance. In another dimension, unification referred to local consolidation of what the administration designated as leadership elites, whose correspondence with genuine indigenous configurations was not always authentic. Most district officers manipulated their respective local elites who commanded assent of their people to various government directives. Local advice was integrated into the decision-making process. However, active and substantive indigenous participation in the central bureaucracy's chain of command did not exist.

In the best spirit of indirect rule, those indigenous administrative elites put numerous other Africans on Native Authority payrolls. But most of those jobs were not fully challenging. Salaries thus integrated these people into the lowest slots on the table of organization. Bloated administrative expenses and many underemployed petty bureaucrats were the costs of local cooperation. Integration, as cross-district or transethnic combinations, was deemed destabilizing and ruled out.

The vertical chain of command and its associated components was a primary unifying agent for the real ruling institution. Affecting the internal operation of the central bureaucracy were kinds of integration resembling those in Native Administration. Consider the functions of the Legislative Council, the Secretariat, and several advisory boards within the context of stability. The Legislative Council, introduced in the mid-1920s, divided into official and unofficial groups. The first included central bureaucrats, including the Governor and department heads. The second, an electoral minority, represented the major unofficial competing bureaucracies in the territory.[5] This was an integration of influential unofficial personalities and groups, but without substantive decision-making power. Even though impact on official decisions was limited, their presence promoted stability. Conflicts between government and unofficial associations or among those latter groups were expressed close to the center of power. Knowing actual or potential friction points within the falsely stereotyped "unofficial alien community" was the prerequisite to minimizing their destabilizing consequences for the bureaucracy.

The true locus of substantive decision-making power was the relationship between Governor and Secretariat, the center's indispensable agency.[6] Governors made the major decisions and bore ultimate territorial responsibility.[7] The Secretariat was responsible for the crucial burdens of information collection, integration, and presentation.

Collecting information from material generated by administrative and technical officers encountered obstacles. The specialized departments never told the Secretariat everything they were doing. Their reports often exhibited the tunnel vision which specialization can foster.[8] Some administrative officers considered themselves above seemingly minor technical details. That attitude sometimes surfaced in the internal records of the Secretariat itself. Generally, the men of the Secretariat knew they needed information that blended administrative with technical considerations and reflected a territorial perspective. Such integrated knowledge was essential to coordinate specialized programs that might, if pursued separately, undermine stability.

A cautious administration created various satellite agencies and special committees to integrate information on one program or industry from a territorial perspective. At least this gave the Secretariat pieces of integrated evidence to consider. In some cases those auxiliary structures expressed important relationships between official and unofficial organization with greater precision than the Legislative Council did.

The Economic and Cotton Advisory Boards demonstrate these more intricate manifestations of stability. Their memberships combined unofficials from specific constituencies with vested interests in a board's subject matter with officials who headed the relevant specialized departments or exercised pertinent general administrative functions. This was such a fine-tuning of unofficial organization that the central bureaucracy changed outside membership on the Cotton Advisory Board to match its shifting perceptions of the relative cohesiveness of the several groups representing middlemen and ginners. These boards gave the most organized unofficials opportunities to influence decisions. Their presence occasionally proved more determinative than advisory. Nonetheless, the Tanganyika administration remained the final arbiter in designing and implementing its own version of economy.

THE BUREAUCRATIC ECONOMY: AXIOMS AND CALCULUS

At least four general axioms influenced the evolving organization of the bureaucratic economy in Tanganyika. The first assumed a divisibility of political economy. The second, third, and fourth axioms represented economic translations of the components of stability—standardization, unification, and integration.

The axiom of divisibility simply meant separating economic from political change in both analytical and practical domains. This separation made possible economic versions of standardization, unification, and integration. Economic standardization meant that the administration spread its own forms for conducting transactions. Introducing East African currency as official money is one example. Economic unification was above all vertical. For example, the existing infrastructure of road and rail, perhaps the most enduring visible feature of the German legacy, facilitated the export of commodities from a particular area more than their local redistribution.

Least important for the bureaucracy was fostering horizontal links among local economic groupings. These unifying ties, which might have engendered an integration of respective structures, posed more immediate threats in the political domain. Cross-district or transethnic communication might ignite combinations of people, groups, and resources that could become alternatives to official indirect rule politics. This unwillingness to unify and integrate the horizontal economic base was a transformation of the stability perceptions which motivated indirect administration. The axiom concerning economic integration should really be understood as the principle of optimal fragmentation of various local levels.

Those axioms provided general guides, but most bureaucrats in Tanganyika knew what they wanted most and least in the realm of economy. There were local variations, but certain objectives were so widely shared that one can construct an administrative calculus of maximization and minimization that may distinguish this version of economy from others.

Increasing revenue was one obvious goal for an administration that depended upon multiple taxes for its own operation. But getting the biggest yield in the shortest time was constrained by more political imperatives. If direct taxation of Africans was too high, it might trigger open displays of discontent, which the bureaucracy sought to avoid. And most bureaucrats preferred above all that Africans work hard, even if such activity was not economically rational. Hard work, defined more by duration than intensity, built "character." It also reduced leisure time that might lead to reflection and the formation of alternative political organization.

The central bureaucracy in Dar es Salaam intersected the tasks of increasing revenue and encouraging hard work. It attempted to coordinate, and often sought to maximize, a third—the regulation of economic activity. There were different modes of manipulation, aimed at goals with varying specificity and complexity. Some embodied a straightforward revenue objective. Some used certain taxes to restrict or inhibit particular kinds of activity. And some reflected the conviction that one could control the rates of political and economic change separately. All modes resulted from pervasive concern with stability in one way or another. The framework of extraction and control which became more intricate over time constituted the core of the bureaucratic economy. Analysis of these sometimes intertwined methods of extraction and control begins with the search for revenue.

2

Servicing the Bureaucratic Economy:
The ABCs of Extraction

E A C H overseas territory should pay its own way as much as possible, according to one British imperial canon. Parsimonious funding from the British Treasury made that principle a daily reality for the Tanganyika bureaucracy. So Tanganyika administrators deployed a range of extractive devices that constituted the bedrock of their own economy. Taxation may not entrance most readers, but the particular mix of levies which this administration employed is significant. Taxation shackled exchange, diverged from what some unofficials and officials wanted, and acquired an overpowering and irreversible momentum often associated with government overregulation. This chapter first presents a partial profile of revenue, then analyzes three important extractive devices—the "native" hut and poll tax, import duties, and railroad rates. A summary vignette shows how once imposed, taxes are not so easily disposed of or reformed.

PROFILING THE WAYS OF EXTRACTION

In the 1920s some members of the Permanent Mandates Commission, which watched over Tanganyika as a Class B League of Nations mandate, protested that they could not understand the territory's financial position based on information in the official budgets. It is easy to empathize with the frustration that motivated those complaints. Reporting categories and procedures changed several times during the inter-war period, hampering comparative evaluation of financial strength or weakness over time. And the administration would not publish certain kinds of detail for understandable reasons. Secretary of Native Affairs Philip E. Mitchell in two private comments noted some political constraints. Writing in his diary for July 15, 1930, he observed that a district-by-district profile of revenue raised from "natives" and disbursements therein "would be gratuitously provocative and would serve to perpetuate racial antagonisms which ought to be allowed to die through inaction."[1] And in 1932, when the Treasurer attempted to estimate the shares of indirect taxes contributed by "natives" and "non-natives," Mitchell was even more pointed: a racial division of revenue and expenditure was a "direct incitement to racial strife" and "politically objectionable."[2] In many budget categories one is left with unrefined aggregates. This level of data may disappoint those seeking quantitative precision, but Tanganyika's territorial budgets were more public relations statements than financial accounting.

Official budgets do show the comprehensiveness of taxation and which taxes were the administration's main money-makers. The partial profile of revenue, table 2.1, and supplementary table, table 2.2, confirm both points.

From fiscal year 1929–1930, one can detail amounts generated by most of those other taxes. Table 2.2 enlarges on that category from table 2.1. In this work I emphasize under the "other" heading those taxes that had an especially constraining impact on many people in Tanganyika. Selected levies fit well with later discussions of regulation: trade licensing fees in chapter 3, the house tax in chapter 4, and various market fees in chapter 5. (Administrators may have put some of those market fees—what people paid to lease markets, for instance—in one or another "miscellaneous" category.) The next two sections examine the two highest-yielding levies—the "native" hut and poll tax and import duties. The third describes an onerous extractive device that the Tanganyika bureaucracy did not consider a tax—the commodity rates imposed by its own railroad administration.

THREE CASE STUDIES OF EXTRACTION

The "Native" Hut and Poll Tax. To understand some effects of the "native" hut and poll tax (after 1936 substitute house for hut), one must first grasp its method of assessment. Direct African taxation employed the district as the key administrative unit and rested on the principle of "ability to pay." A district's ability to pay, as appraised annually by the bureaucracy, set the flat rate for all households within that unit. There were exceptions, as the administration sometimes varied rates within the same district according to one's ethnicity or location. Besides that levy on every household dwelling, the hut and poll tax included a plural wives rate. This component usually averaged about one-half or less of every area's corresponding hut rate, called the "first tax." So the bureaucracy's only fiscal recognition of Africans as individuals came when it counted wives.

TABLE 2.1. PARTIAL PROFILE OF REVENUE: 1924–1938

Year*	Total Revenue (T.R.)	Hut and Poll Taxes		Import Duties**		Other Taxes		Total Taxes	
		Amount	% T. R.	Amount	% T. R.	Amount	% T. R.	Amount	% T. R.
				(pounds)					
1924–25	1,558,982	446,901	28.67	426,725	27.37	85,161	5.46	958,787	61.50
1925–26	1,975,400	674,973	34.17	501,065	25.37	101,228	5.12	1,277,266	64.66
1926–27	2,202,908	682,106	30.96	567,469	25.76	142,463	6.47	1,392,038	63.19
1927–28	1,904,107	708,553	37.21	635,580	33.38	151,899	7.98	1,496,032	78.57
1928–29	1,972,858	736,970	37.36	702,598	35.61	177,203	8.98	1,616,771	81.95
1929–30	1,992,675	748,734	37.57	739,670	37.12	171,235	8.59	1,659,639	83.287
1930–31	1,749,478	700,852	40.06	565,997	32.35	157,865	9.02	1,424,714	81.436
1931–32	1,522,368	537,033	35.28	411,354	27.02	163,964	10.77	1,112,351	73.07
1932 (Apr.–Dec.)	1,290,891	459,428	35.59	299,752	23.22	183,115	14.19	942,295	72.996
1933	1,546,538	590,231	38.16	404,730	26.17	222,160	14.36	1,217,121	78.699
1934	1,720,285	592,119	34.42	476,267	27.69	244,453	14.21	1,312,839	76.32
1935	1,973,863	632,330	32.04	612,563	31.03	265,832	13.47	1,510,725	76.54
1936	2,206,417	657,305	29.79	697,133	31.60	249,184	11.29	1,603,622	72.68
1937	2,345,004	663,241	28.28	751,288	32.04	274,395	11.70	1,688,924	72.02
1938 (est)	2,100,414	630,000	29.99	630,000	29.99	266,840	12.70	1,526,840	72.69

*The bureaucracy changed its fiscal year to coincide with the calendar year in 1932, fully effective in 1933.
**Through fiscal year 1928–29 the author could not disaggregate import duties from excise duties and miscellaneous dues; they were all lumped together in the category "Customs, etc." The latter levies, however, made up only a small fraction of total customs revenue. So the reported figure through 1928–29 slightly overstates the take from import duties.
Sources: Great Britain, Colonial Office, *Tanganyika Territory Reports 1925–1938.*

TABLE 2.2. OTHER TAXES: 1929–1938

| | Licenses | | | House Tax | Non-Native Poll Tax | Non-Native Education | Municipal Tax | Package Taxes | Taxes on Official Salaries | Sugar Tax | Stamp Duties | Excise Duties | Miscellaneous Dues | Miscellaneous Taxes |
Year*	Trade	Vehicle	Miscellaneous											
							(pounds)							
1929–30	58,727	11,629	29,312	29,355	...	...	8,305	...	...	...	17,751	...	4,550	11,606
1930–31	51,688	12,328	24,239	31,082	...	...	8,760	...	...	...	12,947	...	3,827	12,994
1931–32	42,992	12,904	20,666	28,645	...	13,047	8,570	...	10,471	...	10,274	432	2,238	13,725
1932 (Apr.–Dec.)	39,884	7,606	17,639	20,442	29,399	...	12,289	...	32,073	...	7,935	4,849	1,776	9,223
1933	39,553	20,071	20,400	18,904	31,534	...	11,663	412	38,159	8,403	11,041	7,460	2,565	11,995
1934	39,693	22,218	19,693	18,666	35,087	...	11,665	6,587	36,043	11,347	13,221	11,626	3,081	15,526
1935	40,441	25,902	20,056	17,860	37,086	...	10,536	41	31,434	17,292	12,885	21,371	3,044	27,884
1936	43,098	29,795	22,683	1,723	40,482	...	10,466	...	46	14,199	31,537	25,845	3,988	25,322
1937	46,516	34,571	24,870	260	45,241	...	11,230	...	...	22,140	22,555	34,847	4,740	27,425
1938 (est.)	43,000	36,000	23,860	...	46,000	...	12,000	...	...	21,000	20,000	33,000	4,630	27,350

*The bureaucracy changed its fiscal year to coincide with the calendar year in 1932, fully effective from 1933.

The flat rate took as a major indicator the volume of previous tax collections from an area. Most tax officers assumed that extent of collection was an accurate index of past economic activity and the best predictor of future trends. Such a premise was dubious. In 1934 the district officer, Songea, leveled a major if unavailing criticism. He complained, "Hut and Poll tax figures cannot be taken as a very reliable guide, for the methods of collection and assessment may give figures quite irrelevant to the general economic state of the district."[3] The immediate result of this practice was wide variation in flat rates. In 1938, for instance, the "first tax" rate fluctuated from ten shillings on the coast and in the major wage-employment areas to as low as four shillings in some remote locations.[4] These differences produced, in turn, their own effects. Some Tanganyikans were keenly aware of that marked variation and responded by moving into lower-rate locations. The territorial nature of this reaction is difficult to document, but evidence from the southern region indicates its operation there. In 1937 Provincial Commissioner McMahon, Southern Highlands, reported, "Nyakyusa immigration from Rungwe district, particularly along the southern boundary and in the Mbozi area, continues to cause anxiety." He added, "The fear of increasing Nyakyusa immigration on account of low rate of tax was openly discussed."[5] This was a legal and logical mobility, not so much to avoid payment but to remit a lower rate. A more widespread form of movement—territorial labor mobility—gave administrators greater fiscal and social problems.

Imposing an area's flat rate on every African working for wages on alien estates there overlooked the fact that some laborers were outsiders who returned home when they could. Cross-district movement diffused incomes and upset the notion that aggregate district wage-payments all redounded to that unit. This problem eventually compelled bureaucrats to define assessment in relation to location and distribution. Should a worker's tax be based on place of home residence or location of wage-labor? And should that portion of the tax rebated to Native Administration be given to the Authority that administered the district of residence or the district of employment? These were not idle questions. The bureaucracy feared mobility as destabilizing and believed tax policy was a weapon for slowing movement to larger population centers.

The Labour Committee recommended in 1937 that a worker pay tax wherever he is at the rate of his "domicile district" and that the rebate from such taxes go to the Native Treasury of the taxpayer's domicile. Government Circular No. 33 of 1937 implemented these suggestions.[6] Workers paid taxes where they labored, but their place of domicile or residency stayed in effect for two years after leaving home. During that period they were taxed at "home" rates, thereafter at those of the working district. If "home" rates were lower, workers would seem to have a paper incentive for limiting their stay away from home to two years. This harmonized with the administration's objective of reinforcing domestic links, most often rural. But another provision was ambiguous. Should a worker stay away for more than two years, he could re-establish residency in his original home district by a return "of whatever length" necessary to accomplish that goal. How long was enough? Leaving that determination to local authorities, as apparently happened, created uncertainties. The circular refined modes of assessment, but its re-establishment requirement was vague. Workers who stayed in population centers and escaped registration evaded higher rates.

The administration's problem was especially acute in the Tanga district. From that area came most of the sisal, Tanganyika's dominant export during the inter-war period. Alien-managed estates employing African wage earners were a major type of industrial organization. Local staff found it impossible to maximize the hut and poll tax yield there, because at least three factors militated against registration of all taxpayers. District Officer Griffith wrote in the early 1930s about the "mobility of the younger natives," "the impossibility of registering as permanent large numbers of alien natives who live in the district for a while and then move on," and "the proximity of Tanga, where a native may conveniently disappear for a year." Tanga township had become a haven for tax evaders, for there the Native Authority's control broke down and "an attempt to register the natives . . . was given up as impracticable."[7]

Assessment methods, as written and administered, caused certain problems; furthermore, collection modes had an uneven impact on various groups of taxpayers. The Tanga district, with its mix of alien and African enterprise, again illustrates the results. There were three main groups of taxpayers in that area: farmers living in rural locations, "natives" employed in Tanga township, and, of course, the sisal estate laborers. Collectors usually extracted payment from the first two groups in one lump sum, often in and around market centers, and received specie. If some could not pay, they discharged their obligations in labor on public works. The third group encountered different methods of collection, depending on the particular sisal estate. For those workers, a major consideration was whether the tax staff or the estate manager collected payment.

In the 1933 Tanga district report, officers Seymour and Baker noted the difficulties of estate tax collection and asserted that many workers went to an estate where the tax staff, not the manager, was collector. For there "evasion is comparatively simple unless complete co-operation is offered by the Manager which is not generally the case."[8] If caught, "at worst they can be ordered to do a month's work in lieu of the Tax."[9] A worker's selection of that type of estate may also have resulted from the behavior of some tax-collecting managers. At first all such managers had withheld the tax equivalent in cash from each worker's wages, but some had taken advantage of lax bookkeeping requirements and cheated their workers. To reduce those abuses, the administration introduced a system of collection by stamp, which mandated the written certification of withholding. However, this safeguard inspired other forms of misconduct. Every worker should have received a stamped card that verified payroll deductions, yet District Officer Baker reported in 1934 a series of complaints about employers withholding those cards from their employees. Those managers allegedly acted to coerce their workers into new contracts, since ". . . the practice of holding Tax Stamp Cards by the employer has given him a lever to force the labourer to accept a fresh kipande [contract card] on the completion of his old one."[10] How widespread this tactic was is hard to say, but its existence in the Tanga district, a major area of plantation labor, suggests it was more than a casual phenomenon.

With so many assessment and collection problems, direct "native" taxation in Tanganyika garnered attention from all administrative levels. Most passed an unfavorable verdict. The Kitching report, which analyzed Tanganyika's finances, indicted tax rates as too burdensome, deterrents to development in many areas, and stimuli to evasion. Mr. G. Seel, on the Tanganyika desk in the Colonial Office, accepted all these criticisms as persuasive.[11] Major Scupham argued in 1937 that retention of the plural wives tax was a major mistake; this levy "tended to break up native society, since natives [were] no longer willing to become responsible for their deceased brother's wives."[12] And Gov. Harold A. MacMichael had a partial insight into the need for reform, "The main desideratum is to get away from the pre-historic flat tax rate."[13]

While many official critics believed direct "native" tax rates burdensome, some business interests wanted them even higher to "stimulate" increased production for export. This request rested on the erroneous notion that Tanganyikans worked for wages or sold crops for cash only to achieve target holdings, dictated mainly by taxation requirements. In the late 1930s, for instance, Director S. McKnight of the United Africa Company (Tanganyika) Ltd. wrote to the Chief Secretary of the Tanganyika administration and lobbied for an increase in direct "native" taxation to stimulate cash export production. His reasoning was straightforward. "The native in Tanganyika appears to have little interest in production of cash crops except as a means to pay his taxes. For this reason we suggest that Government should carefully consider increased native taxes as a means to inducing them to plant larger quantities of cotton, groundnuts, simsim, etc." Government's official reply was evasive; the Chief Secretary assured McKnight that the administration "will do all in its power to increase production of cash crops." The original draft of that response was more revealing; it contained lines, subsequently removed, which indicate the true attitudes of not only the Chief Secretary but of most other administrative officers. The "best method of inducing increased production of cash crops by natives is not by arbitrarily increasing tax rates"; the preferred techniques were through education and "judicious propaganda" to "raise standard of living of native and to increase his needs so that he will produce more to satisfy those needs."[14]

So the bureaucracy would not raise direct taxes in response to this unofficial pressure. But neither would it substantially overhaul that structure in response to official criticism. Of course, there was some refinement in assessment groupings, some variation in annual rates, and even talk of experimenting with "communal taxation."[15] For all its problems, the "native" hut and poll tax was too entrenched as a major moneymaker and, in most bureaucratic minds, as a pillar of government stability to prompt serious revision. Consider, for instance, its role in local government maintenance and growth. The portion of hut and poll tax revenue annually returned to Native Administrations, which usually averaged between 25 and 30 percent, both sustained existing African personnel and promoted their proliferation. Rebated funds gave each Native Treasury most of its revenue. And administrative expenses, which during the inter-war period supported more and more underemployed petty "native" bureaucrats as noted in chapter 1, accounted for about 65 to 77 percent of total Native Administration spending.[16] Why reform the structure and run a risk of creating greater problems? Besides, underneath the questions of practicality and efficiency, there rankled the theoretical contradictions involved in designing an equitable direct colonial tax.

Import Duties. Revenue generated by import duties remained the second major buttress of administrative financial strength during the inter-war period. The Tanganyika bureaucracy usually tried to maximize the yield from most of those levies but found that an irreversible membership in the East African Customs Union, as well as some internal political factors, constrained its pursuit. (The history of Tanganyika's participation in that Union will not be detailed here because this subject has received attention elsewhere.[17]) The Tanganyika administration, whatever its public pronouncements about the desirability of regional development, became increasingly annoyed during the 1930s at the customs revenue loss that membership imposed. Tanganyika could not increase import duties on overseas commodities beyond a certain level or charge them at all on goods coming from Kenya and Uganda. The bureaucracy attempted to reduce the financial costs of its participation, an endeavor that had several fronts. The first consisted of devising mechanisms for taxing some commodities that should have entered Tanganyika from Kenya or Uganda duty free.[18] A second involved the levying of "suspended duties" on certain overseas commodities. This section concentrates on "suspended duties," because their origin, implementation, effects, and debated revision illustrate the complex considerations Tanganyika administrators faced as they manipulated import duties.

Suspended duties emerged from the deliberations of the 1930 Governors' Conference. The three East African chief administrators then reduced basic import duties on some articles coming from outside the region and appeared to lessen the degree of protection that local producers of those same commodities enjoyed. But each government was permitted to impose an additional duty (not to exceed a prescribed sum) on most affected goods. This was the suspended duty, so called because the extra levy remained "suspended" until each administration in conjunction with its Legislative Council decided to invoke it. The term "suspended," which has misled some scholars, should thus be read "potential."[19] Kenya imposed these duties to the maximum; Tanganyika, in whole or in part on the majority of relevant goods; Uganda, very little. Table 2.3 lists the articles, basic duties, levels of suspended duty permit-

TABLE 2.3.   TANGANYIKA AND SUSPENDED DUTIES

Article	Basic Duty	Suspended Duty	Tanganyika's Decision
Bacon and ham	20% *ad valorem*	10% *ad valorem*	fully imposed
Butter	20% *ad valorem*	10% *ad valorem*	not imposed
Cheese	20% *ad valorem*	10% *ad valorem*	not imposed
Wheat in grain	3/– per 100 lbs	1/50 per 100 lbs	not imposed
Wheat prepared	3/– per 100 lbs	3/– per 100 lbs[a]	1/50 per 100 lbs only
Rice in grain	4/– per 100 lbs	2/– per 100 lbs	fully imposed
Maize in grain	free	20% *ad valorem*	not imposed
Maize meal	free	20% *ad valorem*	not imposed
Ghee	–/30 per lb	–/15 per lb	fully imposed
Sugar (including jaggery)	6/– per 100 lbs	3/– per 100 lbs[b]	6/– in 1931 to 3/– in 1933
Joinery	10% *ad valorem*	20% *ad valorem*	fully imposed
Wood and timber manufactures (except teak)	10% *ad valorem*	20% *ad valorem*	fully imposed

[a]This duty was increased from 1/50 in 1931.
[b]This duty was reduced from 6/– in 1933, a decision discussed in note 18.
Source: Tanzania National Archives Secretariat 26939. Secretary G. K. Whitlamsmith, "Material for an Enquiry into the Effect on the Territory's Economy of the 'Suspended Duties' imposed on certain articles under the Authority of the Customs Tariff Ordinance, 1930, as amended," Central Development Committee Memorandum No. 32, CONFIDENTIAL, May 25, 1939.

ted by the revised 1930 Customs Ordinance, and Tanganyika's decision in each category.

No available records revealed the precise blend of factors that motivated those decisions in every category, but information contained in Secretary Whitlamsmith's memorandum suggests a tentative explanation.[20] Each product or related group of commodities must be considered in turn. A "good deal of bargaining" on duty scales took place among Customs Union participants. Imposing suspended duties fully on bacon and ham from outside the region did help the revenue but was also a concession to Kenya producers of those products. Butter and cheese escaped extra levies, probably because the Tanganyika administration decided placating internal alien consumer preferences was more important than the additional money or again supporting Kenya producers. Differential treatment for wheat in grain and prepared wheat likely came from a decision to protect European wheat farmers in Tanganyika at the more finished stage of production and perhaps to encourage importation of raw wheat for processing. Tanganyika did not take maximum advantage of the suspended duty here, probably because its wheat farmers were neither numerous nor well organized as an unofficial lobby and because local consumer needs for prepared wheat still required outside supplies. Rice in grain obtained maximum protection, since it, along with ghee, constituted Tanganyika's two most important "industries," as described by the Comptroller of Customs. Leaving maize in grain and maize meal duty free recognized implicitly that Tanganyika was a food-deficit territory, unable to produce enough of those commodities to meet local necessities. Treatment of sugar resulted from both the revenue loss axiom and Tanganyika's own initiation of sugar production during this period. The last two categories—joinery and wood and timber manufactures—probably repeat the first—bacon and ham—with respect to rationale.

Even if one had perfect knowledge of inside decision making, the tentativeness of the preceding discussion would not completely disappear. The revenue and protective aspects of suspended duties were open to conflicting interpretations within the Tanganyika bureaucracy itself. The sharpest division of opinion occurred in the late 1930s when the Comptroller of Customs and the Director of Agriculture, among others, debated the revision of suspended duties. The Comptroller recommended their total abolition on multiple grounds: they raised prices for Tanganyika consumers; they supported Kenya with little compensating advantage; and the rice and ghee industries would not be hurt much. He argued that the transoceanic voyage conferred sufficient protection and that Tanganyika lost large sums of money on goods that would otherwise be imported directly from overseas instead of through Kenya. This last point rests on an intriguing variation of the revenue maximization calculus. Since Kenya had imposed suspended duties across the board, Tanganyika could create incentives for overseas interests to ship direct to its ports by opening up more differences in the Union's external tariff wall. This rate reduction would, in the end, produce more revenue, assuming that such differences did influence destination decisions.

The Director of Agriculture had somewhat contrary ideas. He wanted abolition of those duties that protected "native" products (presumably rice, ghee, and jaggery) but retention or increase of those imposed "for the benefit of non-native production (except sugar)." The suspended duty on ghee should go, for instance, because the "native" producer allegedly received such a high price that he would not grow any crops at all and his cattle have gained a "fictitious economic value." But "non-native" products required discriminatory treatment. Director Wakefield argued that the case "for a repeal of the suspended duty on wheat [based on raising standards of nutrition and living] would thus be very strong were it not for its effect upon the wheat growers of Tanganyika Territory." Remove duties and "our young wheat industry is ruined." So far one detects only the "infant industry" argument, but an important stability consideration also lies beneath this plea. Harming the wheat industry would mean that "so many more families in the Arusha area will be a step nearer to becoming 'poor whites,' " a group the emergence of which the administration regarded as embarrassing.[21] While Wakefield's case for retention of the suspended duty on prepared wheat was based on retarding the growth of one group of settlers, his support of the extra levy on bacon and ham was aimed at encouraging others. Retain this duty, he urged, because it will play an important part in the European development of the Southern Highlands and Northern Provinces.

Whitlamsmith's memorandum prepared for the Central Development Committee, which was considering how Tanganyika should develop after 1940, embodied more the Comptroller's views than the Director of Agriculture's. But this tilt did not mean that Wakefield's positions had lost all currency, as argument over suspended duties continued into the 1940s. Such disputes need not be tracked further. The reader can see what considerations impinged on the bureaucracy in levying tariffs and how administrators wrestled with them. Some external interests, though, saw the question of import duties in less complicated terms. For Sir Sydney Armitage-Smith, who toured Tanganyika during the Depression and wrote a report on the territory's finances for the Colonial Office, administrative dependence on a high scale of import duties was disturbing. When the Tanganyika bureaucracy re-established "budgetary equilibrium," he recommended that it decrease indirect taxes, especially import duties. Reduction would "lower retail prices of imported goods to increase native demand for commodities and consequently to stimulate production." Tanganyika's scale of import duties was thus seen as limiting the territory's absorptive capacity for goods coming from outside and as obstructing increased imperial production. With its customary diplomatic acknowledgment of external official admonishment, the Tanganyika administration accepted Armitage-Smith's recommendation "in principle,"[22] but then followed another bit of advice which postponed implementation indefinitely. Achieving and then maintaining "budgetary equilibrium" required the existence of a "safety fund," which Tanganyika administrators believed could best be amassed from general tax revenues.

Railroad Rates. The Tanganyika Railroad Administration, technically an agency of the bureaucracy, imposed high commodity freight rates that evoked almost universal criticism as serious restraints on trade. The following cases can stand as a summary of numerous similar instances. Consider the plight of the European grower in the Northern Province, who found in 1933 that shipping a bag of maize from Moshi to the port of Tanga cost Shillings 1/12, when maize was selling for between 3/50 and 5/- per bag.[23] And note a petition submitted to the bureaucracy in August 1933, by the Lake National Trading Society, an African organization located in Kigoma. This group protested the high freight charges on muhigo (probably *muhogo* or cassava), paddy rice, beans, and dry fish, which amounted to 550/- per wagon load, and sought a return to the previous rate of 250/- per wagon or, at the highest, 300/-. Lake National's petition won preliminary endorsement in the Secretariat from Philip E. Mitchell, who reacted with the incisiveness that characterized so many of his minutes, "I agree with their sentiments entirely and no doubt when we have killed the trade we shall reduce the freight rates." But Acting Chief Secretary E. R. E. Surridge expressed the resignation which was the central administration's final response in this case as well as others, "It is not possible to reduce railway rates as they desire."[24]

Why was the Secretariat so resigned to a schedule of freight rates that constrained trade? The answer lies in the special position of the Railroad Administration within the bureaucracy.[25] This agency had developed a quasi-independence of its own and usually got its way on rate increases. For if Tanganyika were to "pay its own way" and thereby reduce even more the already meager financial assistance it received from the British Treasury, the Railroad Administration had to set an example for other departments of the territorial bureaucracy. Leading the way meant minimizing and then avoiding deficits on the railway account itself, according to strict financial criteria. Any notion of external effects, construed as revenue gains in other tax categories that reduced freight rates generated through incentives to production and trade, was alien to the railroad bureaucracy.

THE MOMENTUM OF OVERREGULATION

One top-level bureaucrat in Tanganyika, Philip Mitchell, evinced special concern about the impact of government overregulation. In 1933 he urged the Economic Advisory Board to investigate the "extent to which restrictions and fees of various kinds have been imposed on trade generally. House tax, municipal tax, market fees, slaughter fees, royalties on forest produce, cesses, licence fees, and so on make up a formidable list." He argued, "All those things reduce the volume of trade and increase the number of officials; indeed we seem . . . to be getting into the frame of mind that if anyone anywhere is making a profit we should tax him and regulate him, and enact legislation about him. And in most cases there is precious little real ground for 'control' except the bureaucratic one that control is in some way desirable in itself, when beyond a certain point taxation withdraws currency from circulation and immobilizes it."

The fate of Mitchell's proposal for a complete review of restrictions and fees shows how powerful the momentum of overregulation can become. The Secretary of the Economic Advisory Board wrote the Chief Secretary and reported that its members felt such an undertaking was "of too great a magnitude" for them to handle. G. J. Partridge, the assistant chief secretary, noted, "This is much too big a subject and that little would result from the appointment of a Committee to go into it." S. B. B. McElderry, the deputy chief secretary, penned the final Secretariat decision: "Let it drop."[26]

I will not let the subject of government intervention in economic activity drop and, in fact, will examine it further in later chapters.

3

Defining Trade and Traders:
The Entrenchment of Economic Inequity

EXTRATERRITORIAL economic connections have so occupied those concerned with the origins of unequal and inequitable exchange relations between developed and developing countries that the internal sources of unbalanced links among different groups of local traders remain improperly appreciated. This chapter, therefore, emphasizes one major internal source by exploring how the Tanganyika administration contributed to the entrenchment of economic inequity or unfairness in relations among various types of local traders, not classified only in racial or ethnic terms. Its contribution came in implementing ordinances and licensing fees that so encumbered exchange that most Africans found it hard to trade on anything more than a small scale. Indeed, the very schedule of licensing fees gave African traders a financial reason for continuing on that low level. This path of cost minimization may have been rational for individuals in the short-run, but the outcome boded ill for the emergence of peer economic relations in the territory. To demonstrate the entrenchment of inequity I will examine the process of administrative ordinance-making and enforcement, and also analyze some criticisms which the bureaucracy received from various contemporaries. The review begins with a glance back at the German record and then considers the first important British legislation.

TRADES LICENSING ORDINANCE OF 1923

Under the German regime, all traders should have paid an industries tax. Government computed this levy in one of two ways: either 4 percent of annual net profits or 0.5 percent of the turnover of the business. Tax laws allowed reasonable allowances for turnover. Fees ranged from 6 to 2,000 rupees for various groups—publicans, innkeepers, restaurant keepers, cattle dealers, pawnbrokers, auctioneers, and commercial agents. In addition, merchants and traders paid an opening fee to open

24

or reopen a shop. This rate varied from 24 to 240 rupees.[1] Under German law, trade was taxed both at its point of original establishment and throughout the life of a business.

In 1923 the bureaucracy enacted a Trades Licensing Ordinance. It retained a profits tax but reduced financial entry barriers for some Africans who wanted to trade on a small scale. This was enough to create some local opportunities. P. E. Mitchell, commenting on the Tanga district for 1923, noted, "The new trades licensing legislation works very satisfactorily; the reduced fee is much appreciated by native traders and is an act of justice to them, which has enabled many to trade in a small way who could not do so before."[2]

It is not known to what extent this reduction was met by a similar fee-elasticity of response and concomitant increase in the legal number of small-scale African traders elsewhere in Tanganyika. What is clear is that P. E. Mitchell's "act of justice" became tarnished. A successful Indian assault on the profits tax, spearheaded by various branches of the Indian business community, led to its repeal in 1927.

Administrators had begun looking for revenue surrogates some time earlier. An advisory committee was appointed by the Governor to "consider the possibility of substituting other sources of revenue for the present profits tax." It concluded at the end of 1926 that to replace lost revenue, increases in trade licensing fees were essential.[3] The Indian Association still remained opposed in principle to "the taxation of trade by means of license fees of any kind."[4] The group agreed with Governor Cameron, who called the imposition of trade licensing fees unusual and noted their disappearance in most countries "on the ground that they are in restraint in trade and are therefore thoroughly unsound."

The Governor argued in late 1925 that such fees existed in Tanganyika for "revenue purposes and the attempt to use them for other purposes, e.g. to force trade into certain channels, cannot be justified." Despite an admission that he could not justify the status quo and a promise "to alter those methods,"[5] Cameron never completely ruled out such fees for revenue purposes. He stated this to Colonial Secretary Amery under confidential cover in 1925.[6] The Indian Association, given a choice between the abolition of profits tax and an increased scale of license fees, had little trouble concluding that "additional revenue could be equitably derived from a revision of trading licences. . . ."[7]

This "equitable" extraction proceeded under a legal framework that was becoming more complicated. The 1923 ordinance employed only one major distinction among the types of trade in its fee schedule. That key difference was between wholesale and retail trade, a difference that depended upon the presence or absence of resale. The Indian Association suggested another contrast—that between importing and exporting or not—and this division worked its way into subsequent legislation, as the Trades Licensing Ordinance of 1927 embodied that double distinction.

TRADES LICENSING ORDINANCE OF 1927

This ordinance provided for the "licensing of persons carrying on businesses." Fees depended upon whether a business was wholesale and "whether or not it includes exportation or importation to or from places beyond the Territory." What was the importance of this second division? The Attorney General saw it as a way to separate the larger and more profitable businesses from the smaller. He acknowledged that this distinction was introduced at the suggestion of a Committee appointed by the Governor, which included representatives of public bodies.[8] However, the significance of the ordinance lies in the design of the fee schedule and its implications.

This scale operated on the premise that the more functions a business exercised and the more numerous its locations, the greater its total fee should be. For example, a wholesale business that also imported from and exported to places outside the Territory purchased a license for 600 shillings. Each subsidiary place of business cost an additional 300 shillings. A wholesale business that did not import or export paid 200 shillings plus 100 shillings for each subsidiary place of business. A retail import business remitted 300 shillings plus 150 for extra places. A non-importing retailer paid 50 shillings. A license that allowed its holder to purchase commodities from "natives" in Tanganyika and sell them within the same territory cost 100 shillings.[9]

This scale of fees, graduated according to size and function, appears progressive because larger and more profitable businesses paid more for their licenses. And the scale applied not only to the initial license, but also to branch fees. Yet it had large loopholes. Once a firm operated within a certain category, it paid only the fees appropriate for that group, no matter what its net profits or turnover. Thus the fee structure within categories was regressive. The smallest business within a particular group paid the same fees as the largest or most profitable in that same classification.

The fee scale also erected a series of escalating financial entry barriers. But administrators took refuge in the fact that this legislation reinforced a special category and fee for African traders. The Acting Attorney General emphasized in April 1927 that a "native carrying on any business other than a wholesale business, or an exempted business, will pay twenty shillings for the principal or only place of business, and ten shillings for each branch business; and, secondly, that clause 13 of the Bill which required traders to keep accounts has been deleted.''[10]

This ordinance set dual standards for admission into the retail without import category, fifty shillings for a ''non-native'' and twenty for a ''native,'' and thereby racialized that classification. On the surface, both special fee and abolition of accounts were designed to help the ''small and semi-literate shopkeeper.'' The same applied to the revised version of the trade license application form which the Governor had rewritten in more straightforward language.''[11]

But this legislation assumed almost no ''native'' upward mobility. To fulfill that axiom, it demarcated higher business categories with larger fees. This put entry out of reach for those who had trouble coming up with even twenty shillings for a ''native'' license. Entry barriers for each category of business, whether laterally or from below, were many. They included such hurdles as minimal start-up, maintenance, and perhaps expansion capital, a network of connections inside and outside the territory, and markets sufficient to support the activities of new entrants.

This does not mean the financial barriers posed by entry costs were insuperable obstacles but does suggest that the ladder of rising entry costs was one reason for the excessive concentration of African traders on the lowest rungs. The problem for many in Tanganyika was not just the acquisition of adequate capital to sustain one's activity, but the basic necessity of obtaining means to crack the financial entry barriers.

ITINERANT TRADERS ORDINANCE OF 1927

The second of three related 1927 trade ordinances focused on the problem of the itinerant trader.[12] In its initial dimension the problem had been one of definition, which this legislation contained. What prompted classification was a difficulty of fitting the then predominant trade categories to everyone's activity. In January 1927 the Treasurer called the Chief Secretary's attention to the fact that ''there is a distinct class of native traders in the Territory, far more numerous than pedlars, who travel around districts, either as agents, or on their own behalf, buying produce from the peasantry.''

How should these people be identified? The Treasurer continued, ''As a result of paragraph 3 of General Notice No. 160 of 1923, it is the practice to class these traders as pedlars but it will be seen from paragraph 5 of your circular memorandum No. 146/3/15 of 12 July 1923 that the Notice in question does not apply if purchases are made for cash (as they often are) and it is confusing and illogical that the same form of trading should be governed by different ordinances as to whether purchases are made by barter or cash.''

He then suggested that the Pedlars and Livestock Dealers Ordinance be amended to include itinerant traders and to regulate sales whether by barter or cash. These proposals came from the "need to regularize" as well as the desirability from an administrative and revenue point of view of placing "these itinerant buyers under the conditions as to the carrying of licenses, apprehension, etc. as apply to itinerant vendors."[13]

The Secretariat responded that the proposed solution was not very useful, because if a trader only bought produce for cash, he was not a pedlar, and, therefore, a revision of the Pedlars' Ordinance was misplaced.[14] Itinerant trading thus got its own legislation, which defined an itinerant trader as "any person who either on his own behalf, or as an agent for another person, travels from place to place selling . . . or offering to buy. . . ." The object of this ordinance was to control those traders without definite premises. As a first step it mandated that each trader so defined take out a license that cost twenty shillings.[15]

This ordinance was only a beginning. Itinerant trading activated several administrative biases simultaneously. The first was a widespread dislike of traders and perhaps even of most business people.[16] The second came from bureaucratic stability requirements. And as the bureaucracy moved to organize more official stationary markets, itinerant trading gained more disapproval. The effects of official market organization on mobile businesses and other economic activity are analyzed in detail in chapter 5. As an introduction, consider an excerpt from a Legislative Council debate at the second reading of the 1928 Markets Bill.[17] This bill added some geographical restrictions to the control web enveloping itinerant traders.

Three unofficial members argued against the legislation and advanced several criticisms. Ruggles-Brise, Boyd-Moss, and Lead asserted that it discriminated against the country in favor of the town. And, to the extent that markets concentrated around population centers reduced the territorial dispersion of exchange, they would be right. All three suggested that only the local Exchequer would benefit; the bill was not designed to foster development. Major Lead elaborated, "It is really only a matter of market revenue which we are now considering; that is the only practical point. I do not think that this point is of sufficient importance to pass legislation which undoubtedly might tend to interfere with the free movement of produce.''

However accurate these observations, the bureaucracy remained unpersuaded. The Provincial Commissioner, Eastern, furnished the government reply. This bill, he stated, was aimed at itinerant traders who establish temporary sites within a mile or so of approved markets in districts outside townships.[18] His rejoinder did not really contradict Lead's point, because itinerant traders did siphon off trade and related revenues from government-approved market sites.

As some officials pushed bulk marketing in the 1930s, itinerant trading reached its nadir on the bureaucracy's ranking of acceptable small-scale exchange activities. On February 23, 1931, Secretary of Native Affairs P. E. Mitchell recorded in his diary a discussion he had with Director of Agriculture Harrison, ''. . . I said I had come round to the view that itinerant trading must be stopped in the interests of crop quality and bulk marketing. That is his view in any case.''[19] In a 1934 Legislative Council debate Mitchell conceded, ''. . . the small trader has spread . . . in the interior the manufactured goods which are the primary incentive to production.'' At the outset, ''he traded largely by barter and in small quantities of native produce.'' But ''that system has . . . served its purpose and is no longer suited to the conditions in which we live. . . .''

Organized bulk marketing was the solution to changing conditions, but there was still a role for the small trader if only that person would settle down and conduct business in a fixed location. It was essential, Mitchell concluded, to separate ''the business of retail shopkeeping from the totally different business of bulk marketing of peasant crops in standard and dependable grades with the smallest possible overhead charges.''[20]

Bulk marketing and cooperatives will be considered in chapter 8, but readers can now see all the forces working against itinerant traders.

THE 1932 LEGISLATIVE TRIAD

In 1932 administrators implemented refined versions of three ordinances as a comprehensive approach to several exchange problems that had grown more nettlesome. This threesome—Trades Licensing (Amendment) Bill, the Markets (Amendment) Bill, and the Itinerant Traders (Amendment) Bill—aimed at consolidation and the concomitant reduction of small-scale operations. All three further defined a controlled situation in which the bureaucracy hoped to increase revenue. This section concentrates on two significant features of the amended Trades Licensing Bill because both the revised Itinerant Traders Bill[21] and Markets Bill[22] tightened the familiar control web surrounding itinerant trading.

In its first important provision the Trades Licensing (Amendment) Bill mandated that all transactions employ official East African shillings and cents, the bureaucracy's money. This injunction originated in the administration's double perception of a dwindling cash circulation and an increasing spread of barter, circumstances which threatened tax collections. The author has elsewhere analyzed various perceptions of money and barter in inter-war Tanganyika and demonstrated some harmful consequences from enforcing rigid media categories.[23] So here the focus is on clashing official and unofficial views of what this cash provision meant for trade and traders. The Legislative Council debaters speak for themselves.

Two Indian members, Chitale and Malik, entered strong protests. Neither spoke without bias, but both were correct: compelling the use of cash would hamper exchange because cash was short.[24] Major Lead strengthened this argument, although in the end he supported the bill. Barter was not necessarily bad in an economic sense, particularly during the Depression. It was the "function of the up-country trader to do quite a lot of barter," Lead suggested. Much coin was ending up in bank strong rooms every week and "becoming less productive up country." In short, it might be impossible to move stocks except in return for produce.[25]

Director of Agriculture Harrison rejoined that compulsory cash transactions would produce more cash in a district and, as a result, the small trader would "have more chance of selling his stock." How this scenario would work is not clear. Harrison himself admitted, "It is rather difficult to state what exactly will be the effect of this Ordinance. I am hoping, sincerely hoping, that it will add to the prosperity of the native peoples, to the increased production of more and better kinds of produce, and by means of the other two ordinances [Itinerant Traders and Markets] . . . establish traders and markets more soundly."[26]

The second significant feature of the revised Trade Licensing Ordinance was the exclusive trade license. Harrison had proposed this device to a Government House Conference on Tax (Hut and Poll) in December 1931. He justified such a license for the introduction of a new crop that needed "careful buying on grade and a particular type of material to be grown." Its purpose was "to check competition for native crops which cause great fluctuations in price."[27] The exclusive trade license would have eliminated competition altogether by permitting its holder to purchase a specific crop in a definite location for a fair price set by the bureaucracy. Administrative attitudes towards prices and the "plant-more-crops" campaign will be discussed in chapter 6.

Contemporary critics of exclusive licenses and cash transactions sometimes scored general bureaucratic approaches to trade and traders. They came from many backgrounds. Captain Rydon, an unofficial member of the Legislative Council, asserted that "exclusive trade license" was only a cover for monopolies. These were bad because the monopolist tends to pay the lowest price and sell at the highest and "that, in my opinion, is bound to react adversely against the native." Rydon thought the "native" a "funny fellow where trade is concerned," for "he has his own ideas as to what a fair price is, and if he does not get that price he does not produce." Although Rydon did not oppose the bill, he asked that the monopoly issue be considered: "I am very much afraid that if we allow these monopolies he [the "native"] will be the loser."[28] More strident opposition came from the Indian Association, which argued that exclusive licenses contravened Article 7 of the Mandate, forbidding unequal commercial opportunities.

Mixed reactions emanated from the Colonial Office. Looking at the entire legislative package, G. Seel conceded that it was difficult "not to approach these three Ordinances with a feeling of dislike, as they represent two ideas, viz. the attempt to enforce restrictions upon trading and the attempt to make cash the sole medium of business transactions, which might have been supposed to have been killed by the study of political economy."

Still, he hoped that these ordinances would control trade and make efforts to increase "native" output worthwhile. He even offered a rationale for supporting the triad: compulsory cash transactions diffused a common standard of value. Unless sales were for cash, the bureaucracy could not assess the fairness of prices.[29] And a cash standard was essential, according to J. F. N. Green, because barter gave "the Indian trader a double opportunity of swindling."[30]

Seel further believed that the exclusive trade license might encourage the "native producer to improve the quality of his crop," now "frustrated by the practice of small merchants (in nearly all cases Indians) who pay the same price for good, bad, or indifferent produce." He found complaints from the Indian Association irritating but not compelling: "The exclusive licenses are to be given for definite areas and can therefore hardly be regarded as general monopolies in the sense of Article 7 of the Mandate."[31] These reasons wilted somewhat under criticism from Phillip Cunliffe-Lister, then Colonial Secretary. Why must the license be exclusive, he asked, since it was hard to enforce fair play under a system of even minor monopolies [monopsonies], which "by stifling competition might actually reduce prices to native growers." "The governing principle," he argued, "should be to adapt the machinery of administration to fit the actual conditions of trade and not attempt to canalize trade so as to facilitate the task of administration."[32]

Nonetheless, reluctant Colonial Office endorsement came when the

Tanganyika bureaucracy promised to limit severely the introduction of the exclusive license.[33] To this pledge administrators remained faithful during the 1930s, perhaps because of their judiciousness. More likely it was on account of the pressure that the Indian Association exerted on any prospective applicant to cease such endeavors and on actual holders to surrender their licenses.[34]

EVALUATION IN THE MID-1930s

In 1935 the Governor appointed a committee to examine trades licensing legislation.[35] Its report evoked various official and unofficial reactions, some of which illuminate the ground-level fate of different groups of traders. This section will consider that document, the responses it provoked, and the minor alterations it promoted. Although this procedure had marginal effects on policy direction, it gave many a chance to speak critically about the premises and results of decisions.

In its major recommendations, the Committee endorsed with minor revisions the status quo in all important respects except one. It concluded, first, that the general form of the ordinance should remain unchanged but that the scale of fees should be made exclusive and so contain no such item as "any other trade," a phrase which had caused difficulty in the past.

Considering whether to retain the present wholesale-retail distinction or adopt the Kenya system of graduated fees in relation to value of stocks held, the Committee decided to stick mainly with the former for two reasons: "In a territory in which by far the greater portion of the trade is in the hands of Asiatics any system calling for inspection of stocks and books would present many difficulties"; and licensing officers and traders were "familiar with the *status quo.*"[36]

In this second area, retention included suggestions for more rigorous definitions. "Import" should designate goods brought from anywhere outside the Territory. But it should not include country produce from a place covered by the Customs Agreement. "Export" should refer to locations "outside area of Customs Agreement, but not including Zanzibar." "Retail" trade should denote "habitual sale" of goods direct to the consumer. The fourth major category, "wholesale" trading, received only partial specification: ". . . the first principle of wholesale trading was the habitual sale of goods to the trader for the purpose of re-sale."[37]

The crucial exception came in its third major recommendation. The Committee proposed to "eliminate racial discrimination" by abolishing special "native" trading licenses. Disappearance of the 20/- license would have made "natives" liable to pay, in some instances, a 100/- fee. The Committee offset this increase to some extent with a motion to incorporate the principle of graduation in a limited fashion. It asked for the creation of a two-tier license structure for the business of retail trader (excluding imports and exports). For a trader whose stock exceeded 30 pounds (600 shillings) during the licensing period, a license would cost 50/-; for one whose stock never went above 30 pounds, a certificate would carry a 20/- price tag.[38]

How did these recommendations fare? The bureaucracy agreed that the general form of the ordinance was acceptable but disputed the desirability of exclusive categories. Both the law officers and the Secretariat opposed too much precision. The Attorney General remarked, ". . . it is dangerous to repeal and re-enact for many reasons; e.g., to do so will enable the Leg Co. to discuss matters which are controversial i.e. Part II of the existing Ordinance: furthermore the structure of the existing Ordinance is empirical but it works . . ." He was a "little apprehensive of the effect on the structure of the existing Ordinances of introducing attempts at exact definitions: this is one reason for retaining the existing exemptions and the power to make further exemptions: this retention is inconsistent with the principal [sic] of exclusiveness but without exemptions the definitions are much too wide e.g., a farmer selling his stock or a planter selling his crop are wholesale traders within the definitions but it is not intended that they should take out licenses."[39]

The 1936 amended law exempted a range of transactions.[40] Bureaucrats accepted the second recommendation and in the amended 1936 fee schedule sharpened the double distinctions of wholesale-retail and export-import, according to the Committee's suggestions.

But administrators rejected abolishing the special "native" trading license and introducing any fee graduation by stock value. The Secretariat had canvassed local officers for criticism of the official committee proposals and the most adverse commentary centered on abolition. The Acting Provincial Commissioner, Lake, stated in 1936 that the report "summarily dismissed the Native's claim to a license at a lesser rate than a non-native" and on the "encouragement of native trading, the Committee are unanimous to the contrary." If the document were fully implemented, it would "have the effect of almost entirely eliminating the native produce buyer." There were 633 African traders licensed to buy coffee in Bukoba in 1935 plus 862 itinerant African coffee buyers. The former would have to pay 100/- for a license.

This prediction was ominous, since the presence of certain types of African traders relieved the administration from other sorts of pressures. The Acting Provincial Commissioner forecast two specific effects of reduction or elimination. The first was expected: "grave discontent to these people." The second was more threatening: "it may also have the effect of hastening the formation of co-operative societies and with it 'bulk' marketing which at this stage does not appear desirable in my opinion."[41]

Conjuring up visions of multiplying cooperatives was one way to unsettle some administrators in the 1930s (chapter 8). What mix of fears influenced the status quo decision here is unknown. In its official rejection, the bureaucracy stated that acceptance would have "involved making the native pay 100/– for a license to purchase from a native the produce of the territory, or reducing the fee for this license to that paid by the native: this was felt to involve a loss to revenue which Government could not face."[42]

During the drafting process the Dar es Salaam Indian Association had incisively criticized the suitability of even the refined definitions of wholesale and retail. Its Executive Committee submitted a detailed memorandum that deserves credibility in spite of its bias. This judgment comes from the fact that the memorandum amplifies a problem understated before in official government reports. District Officer A. V. Hartnoll, Dodoma, pinpointed that problem in his 1927 submission. Postscripting the almost automatic assessment that "the new trades licensing legislation introduced at the beginning of the year has been working well," he noted that "the only difficulty has been in differentiating between the wholesale and retail trader."[43] That "only difficulty" became an important problem that irritated some bureaucrats and truly upset many traders.

Why were the definitions so discordant in practice? Wholesale and retail did not, the Executive Committee argued, "interpret the true state of transactions in the bazaar." The crux of that distinction rested on whether or not a trader resold his merchandise to another trader, not a final consumer. The Executive Committee observed that there were many mixed cases, when a commodity was partially used by the buyer for himself and the rest resold: "In small places, particularly, it is most usual that a duka owner [shopkeeper] will buy from a neighbouring retailer a packet of match boxes for re-sale to a customer, or he may partly buy for his own use and partly he may re-sell." In fact, "such are the transactions which are most common and over which the retailer can have no control, but under the definition of retail he would be liable as a 'wholesale merchant.'"

Draft definitions proposed by the official committee, which essentially duplicated earlier versions, "can apply to a highly developed country where the volume of wholesale transactions is very high and not in this

Territory where the distinction is very difficult to check and liable to be misused by the executive to harass the trading community." For the Indian retailer, and likely the African retailer, "to determine to whom he is selling—to the consumer or re-sale—is a proceeding impossible of determination and at any rate beyond the control of the retail merchant."[44]

The harassment made possible by that wholesale-retail distinction is significant. The Executive Committee cited the case of a retail merchant in the Rufiji district who held a 100 shilling license and was prosecuted for selling four kilos of kerosene oil to a "native" whom the police identified as a shopkeeper. This was a "frivolous" case and ruinous to the small trader who had no knowledge of the buyer's background, the Committee argued; in this case the merchant should have had a wholesale license costing 200 shillings.

It is difficult to determine how widespread prosecutions of this sort were.[45] If the bureaucracy was right, the episode was "an abuse—not part of the system."[46] But the chilling effects rising from possible prosecution could only hamper exchanges between people whose backgrounds were not known to each other and retard peer integration between Indian and African trading communities. To avoid prosecution, the Indian retailer most likely sold to the African as final consumer, not as a fellow retailer.

This legal onus thus inhibited the formation of horizontal links between groups of similar occupation. Consider the circumstances of an African retailer forced to find an Indian wholesaler. Especially for the up-country African this necessity, made even more difficult by the clustering of wholesalers around population centers,[47] increased transactions costs by adding more transport expenses, consumed more of the African retailer's time, and perhaps reduced the ultimate dispersion and availability of consumers' goods. So the Executive Committee offered revised definitions. A retail business involved sale of goods in broken packages or in quantities not equal to or greater than an unbroken package, excluding hawking. "Unbroken" characterized a package as it was when first imported into Tanganyika or "according to the trade custom in each particular case." Retail was, therefore, not defined from the standpoint of the consumer or resale, but in terms of bulk or quantity. The wholesale definition followed accordingly.[48]

These suggestions were, of course, rejected outright. Treasurer Sandford commented that although the basic definitions "are by no means unassailable under present practice," they "are reasonably well understood and may be regarded as preferable to any suggested alternatives on that account alone." An argument based on widespread assumptions actually rested on the fear that greater congruity between category and reality might diminish revenue; he might favor "some far-reaching amendments to the present Trades Licensing Law if the fiscal system in Tanganyika was on such a basis as justified Government in abandoning this law as a measure designed to secure substantial revenue, but that position has not yet been reached and in spite of the return to prosperity, I cannot recommend that the revenue aspect of the present law should be over-looked."[49]

So ended a revision that produced much substantive criticism but only minor changes.[50] Reform boded revenue loss and instability, and the basic licensing structure remained intact—with its unbalanced blend of progressivity and regressivity, its somewhat unrealistic definition of exchange forms embodying a significant prosecutorial threat, and its almost perverse encouragement of African traders to take the path of minimization by keeping the twenty shilling license, which reinforced their concentration on the lowest rungs of the retail category. Now all Africans found their ability to engage in anything beyond small-scale exchange with limited time horizons restricted by the administration's credit policy.

4

Restricting African Access to Credit: The Enlargement of Dependent Opportunity

T H E Tanganyika administration attempted to prevent the growth of credit markets for many Africans and hedged existing markets with restrictions. These led to practices which strengthened the dependence of some Africans on Indian business people. Why bureaucrats so acted, what their definitions of credit and collateral were, and how implementation suffocated economic opportunities for some and fostered dependency for others are major concerns in this chapter. It begins with the general origins and strategy of the administration's approach, then considers its formulation, impact, and refinement. Important implications are summarized at the end.

ORIGINS AND STRATEGY

General credit policy had five origins: an assumption about desirable exchange evolution influenced by revenue needs, perceptions of Asiatic commercial avarice and African naiveté, the lobbying effectiveness of Indian organizations, the Mandate's injunctions concerning usury, and the related fears concerning agricultural debt and a landless peasantry. All five origins are important. The first three were introduced in the previous chapter; they will be amplified here before the last two are presented.

Official cash was the preferred medium for taxes so it had to be diffused. However, most administrators viewed credit as the kind of transaction that should predominate only in the most advanced stage of economic maturation. Territories and individuals reached this stage only after an apprenticeship of an unspecified duration in the official cash economy (stage two) had reduced or eliminated the primitivism of barter (stage one). Forestalling stage three—the credit economy—was the other front in the drive to enforce use of colonial legal tender. This area has remained less explored because the first front—suppressing barter—was more overtly destructive.

A second motivation for the credit policy was the official perception, largely stereotyped, of greedy Asiatic business people exploiting unsuspecting "natives." An anti-commercial bias (which P. E. Mitchell put with such vitriol in chapter 3 notes) sometimes took specific forms. In 1920 Captain Frank Hallier, then district officer, Rufiji, revealed the thoughts of many administrative officers, when he described the "native" as "at the mercy of the Asiatic trader, who grows rich, while [the "native"] often has difficulty in feeding and clothing himself and his family." [1] One root of this imbalance, Hallier believed, was the "undesirable practice of encouraging the natives to incur large debts on credit," which was "nothing short of criminal." [2]

But those whose encouragement was allegedly "criminal" found themselves indirect targets in credit legislation. This came, in part, from the Indian associations' effective protests whenever the administration contemplated too close inspection of their daily business practices. Their lobbying, though never threatening administrative hegemony, still challenged the bureaucracy's tranquillity enough to discourage direct legislative attack. They also owed their partial reprieve to the situation in inter-war Tanganyika that administrators had faced when considering how to implement Article 6 of the British Mandate for East Africa.

The third paragraph of that article enjoined the Mandatory to "promulgate strict regulations against usury." [3] The article did not enlighten the Tanganyika administration; it neither defined usury nor specified enforcement. What constitutes the difference between usury and an adequate compensation for risk incurred and services rendered is sometimes a very fine line. Moreover, it is a distinction that can shift suddenly as market conditions change. Defining usury, drafting practical legislation, and then enforcing it—all these problems would have bedevilled administrators had they not encountered insuperable barriers right away. Most Asiatic business people did not keep records in English, if they kept them at all. These facts made it hard to apply a standard definition of profit; the bureaucracy conceded this in its repeal of the Profits Tax Ordinance, mentioned in the last chapter. These information and language barriers also militated against constructing a schedule of fair interest rates based on the East African currency system, an unrealistic project that never got under way.

The final impetus for credit policy was fear. Some administrators were concerned that Africans had borrowed too much with their land pledged as collateral and that those who defaulted would enter the ranks of a landless peasantry, thus threatening stability. These fears were perhaps not as central to the original formulation of credit legislation as the first four factors were. But in the 1930s some bureaucrats developed them as major justifications for their narrow practical definitions of collateral.

For all these reasons the administration adopted the straightforward strategy of restricting African access to credit. The premise was comprehensive. Reducing the number of credit transactions retards stage three, contracts the potential incidence of undesirable Asiatic commercial behavior, protects the "natives," and ensures the stability of the ruling institution.

CREDIT TO NATIVES (RESTRICTION) ORDINANCE OF 1923:
INCOMPLETE DEFINITIONS, CONTROVERSIAL IMPACT,
AND PRESSURE FOR REVISION

The Credit to Natives legislation of 1923 defined credit as a debt. Its third section prescribed, "No debt for money lent or goods supplied by a non-native after the commencement of this Ordinance shall be recoverable from a native unless—(a) the transaction creating the debt is in writing and approved in writing by an administrative officer; or (b) the native holds a permit in writing from an administrative officer to contract such debts without the approval of an administrative officer." Its fourth section mentioned collateral: "No security, including a bill of exchange or promissory note, given by a native shall be enforceable or realisable, either by a court or out of court, for the payment of a debt which by virtue of this Ordinance is irrecoverable."[4]

Neither credit nor collateral received exhaustive description, an imprecision which the administration preferred. Credit does in one sense denote a "debt due in consequence of a contract of hire or borrowing of money," and in another "the time allowed by the creditor for the payment of goods sold by him to the debtor." But in a still more fundamental sense, one which the Ordinance ignores, credit means the "ability to borrow, on the opinion conceived by the lender that he will be repaid."[5]

The passage of that Ordinance both satisfied need and raised hope. In 1923 then District Officer P. E. Mitchell, Tanga, wrote, "The Credit to Natives Ordinance fills a long felt want and will do more than anything else to prevent the African from selling or encumbering his land."[6] Eight years later, Secretary of Native Affairs Mitchell saw the fulfillment of his own prophecy. "The present Ordinance has worked well," he concluded, adding, "There is no hardship whatever in requiring shopkeepers to abstain from giving credit to natives. . . ." Indeed, the Secretary believed, "If there were Africans in the Leg. Co. [Legislative Council] they would all oppose any relaxation of the Bill."[7] Governor Cameron was as confident of his ability to divine "native" intentions. He doubted "if the natives want a great deal, if any, credit facilities; what they want is assistance in co-operative selling, i.e. secured markets, so far as markets can be secure."[8]

Some unofficial descriptions of economic behavior and assessments of impact were more realistic. At the second Legislative Council reading of the Bankruptcy Bill in 1930, Mr. Chitale told his fellow members, "We all know that in spite of that Ordinance [1923 Restriction of Credit] a great deal of credit is given to natives without the sanction of the District Officer." Although the law had not stopped credit transactions, its provisions were affecting commercial relations in various ways. Chitale spoke about and perhaps exaggerated the fate of some Indian business people, "The small trader goes bankrupt as a result of the credit to natives which he knows is irrecoverable, and as a result the only asset which he possesses is a small quantity of goods and a lot of boxes deposited with him by labourers."[9] Some administrators might have remained content to relish this as lenders' just punishment had not powerful pressures for legislative revision begun to peak. The spokesmen for change came not only from Indian organizations but also from the European representation on the Legislative Council. They concentrated, among other things, on winning exemptions from the 1923 Ordinance for African traders and built their case, in large part, on harms generated by the irrecoverability provisions.

In February 1930, two European members on the Legislative Council argued for exempting African traders and, at the same time, enriched an emerging portrait of economic behavior and legislative impact. Mr. Boyd-Moss spoke about the "serious disability a native will be under if he is not allowed to obtain goods on credit," as "most of the trade in this country is done on the credit system and a small trader gets all his goods on credit and sells them before he pays for them." Boyd-Moss added, "No firm is going to advance goods to a native if they cannot think that they are likely to obtain the money for those goods afterwards. Consequently, it is the native who will suffer."[10] Boyd-Moss appears to contradict Chitale's testimony on evasion, but if he is talking about European firms and not small-scale Indian traders, there is no conflict.

Most significant, though, is their concurrent interpretation of some practical reactions to the Ordinance. Who had time to seek out an administrative officer and his approval every time one needed credit? (The author could find no instances of general permits issued under Section

3b.) What if an applicant knew little or no English and the district officer had an imperfect grasp of Kiswahili or the prevailing local languages, and no competent translators were available? How would a creditor who knew little or no English react to a document of permission written in that language? What if neither debtor nor creditor could write their most likely common language, Kiswahili, let alone English, and thus not make a legal transaction? Why would a debtor who could not read a creditor's written statement enter into an agreement that might be loaded against him? And so on.

Most people thus lent facing the possibility of loss with no legal recourse or, inhibited by administrative red tape, did not grant any credit to Africans at all. The 1923 Ordinance was, therefore, restricting more than Africans. However, it was on the issue of exempting African traders that Major William Lead, another European member of the Legislative Council, pushed administrators. He noted, "Certain natives are becoming more sophisticated and really entering the realms of trade . . . the very fact of having to take out that license should automatically remove them from the protection afforded by the Native Credit Ordinance."[11]

The Tabora Indian community sought a more sweeping objective— repeal of the Ordinance. Its effects were "disastrous" and prevented "the growth of commercial relations which are necessary for this Territory." That group specified, "If some protection [were] necessary to the Natives of this Territory, in their dealings with Non-Natives, the Indian Community suggest that an Act similar to the Usurious Loans Act of India should be made applicable to all commercial transactions so that, the Courts could go through any transaction whatever be the form the transaction takes and set it and if it were inequitable."[12]

And the *Tanganyika Standard,* which spoke for some Indian business interests, editorialized that it was impossible "to visualize the development of the African to higher moral and intellectual standards if in his earliest stages of development, he is to be placed on this pinnacle, a Lord Paramount, with no obligations to society, no inspiration to responsible citizenship, and no urge whatever to industry."[13] These Indian opinions cannot be dismissed as special pleading altogether, although calling for a usury act on the India model was unrealistic. To restore legal recoverability was in their best interests. But the equal liability of all to court action was also necessary for the evolution of peer commercial relations among different groups and individuals in the territory.

Exempting African traders was just one of the changes administrators contemplated as they reconsidered the basic Ordinance during 1929 and 1930, although repeal was never a serious option.

CREDIT TO NATIVES (RESTRICTION) ORDINANCE OF 1931:
PAPER REVISIONS, PRACTICAL GUIDELINES, AND
NARROWED MEANINGS OF COLLATERAL

The Credit to Natives Ordinance of 1931, the major inter-war revision of credit legislation,[14] contained four principal changes—one was an addition; three were exemptions. Added to the irrecoverable debt category were services of a professional nature (excluding medical practitioners); such debts were irrecoverable unless a district officer approved the transaction in writing or the "native" held an exemption permit. Excluded from the provisions were trading contracts made by "natives" holding trading licenses. Those advocates for exemption had succeeded. Chief Secretary D. J. Jardine, paraphrasing Major Lead's words, explained, "If a native is sophisticated enough to take out a trading license, he should know how to honour his trading obligations."[15] Also removed from the law's protection were Somalis and Abyssinians, because these people "were sufficiently astute and competent to conduct their business affairs unfettered by formalities and without the measure of protection which is considered necessary in the case of native Africans."[16]

The third exemption affected "any loans to native servants," which took the form of an advance on wages not exceeding the sum of one month's wages and the amount of hut and poll tax owed by the worker. This provision, which may seem another concession, had gained support as a way to limit a ready source of credit for some African workers. The Reverend R. M. Gibbons, who supposedly represented African interests on the Legislative Council, was "delighted to learn that there is a definite limit put on any loan a native may obtain. It is important that he should be taught to live on his wages as far as possible." Gibbons argued, "The native at the present does not understand money; a few of the coast natives may do so, but the vast majority do not; but as long as they think they can get an easy loan they will go on borrowing."[17]

One significant exemption proposed—but rejected—concerned those recognized as legitimate chiefs by the bureaucracy. In June 1929, Governor Cameron quashed this motion, "I am much opposed to any relaxation of the law at present."[18] Restrictions on credit to chiefs reinforced their financial dependence on official salaries, giving them a vested interest in the present system. When the revised ordinance gave Africans a chance to buy some relief by purchasing a trade license, the administration removed that option for its indigenous leaders and even prevented any already trading from continuing in both roles. Gov. Stuart Symes reported to his East African colleagues in 1933, "We have had only one case of a Chief being a trader, and we then informed him that he could be one or the other but not both: he closed his store. We should certainly take the same view in any future cases.[19]

The revised ordinance conferred its most important deregulation on African traders holding licenses, as well as on those who might obtain a license and be able to justify their transactions as falling within a trading contract. But the ability to borrow rests, in part, on the legality of collateral. Creating a more equitable regulatory environment for those groups would mean little, unless their assets qualified as legal collateral. And if there were obstacles to certification of assets as collateral, then non-exempted Africans would experience even more difficulties in obtaining credit.

There were significant obstacles. These stemmed, in large measure, from a definition of collateral or security. The definition seemed elastic in legislation but then narrowed when administrators interpreted it on paper. It became impossibly tight in practice. The 1923 Ordinance had partly defined security as "a bill of exchange or promissory note" and left room for further enumeration. But most administrators would have agreed with Governor Symes, when he wrote in 1933, "The only security which a native possesses is as a rule his land and in some cases cattle."[20] One major problem for borrowers was that the bureaucracy sometimes required the possessor to prove ownership, an especially complicated task in this context. The Land Act of 1923 had disavowed private ownership, asserted that the Governor held all land in the territory in trusteeship for its inhabitants, and prescribed that land be distributed on the basis of leaseholds. Had there been no colonial land law, Secretary Mitchell's characterization would still have applied to many Africans in some asset categories, including land. He said, ". . . the great [administrative] difficulty is that the assets of a native, or at least those assets upon which any creditor can distrain, are generally speaking not his individual property at all."[21]

But the administration persisted. In 1932 the Secretariat instructed local officers as to how to treat applicants who were seeking relaxation of the Credit Restriction Ordinance and who wanted to borrow money on immovable property. Chief Secretary Jardine admonished officials to "exercise great care" to prove that an applicant is the "legal owner of property," that "there are no other owners or occupiers," and "in particular that a single heir in a joint undivided Mohammedan estate is not thus enabled to raise money by mortgaging property in which others have an interest, without their knowledge."[22] A non-exempted potential borrower who presented land as collateral would thus encounter crushing obstacles. Proving his ownership within prevailing local customs may have been impossible. And even if it were, such a bond would have placed him in technical violation of colonial land law.

Those recently exempted also found their ability to use land as collateral restricted. Governor Symes observed in 1933, "A native trader might of course endeavour to secure a loan on his land but I think the Land Officer would now successfully intervene and prevent its attachment and sale," as "transfer to a non-native requires the Governor's sanction, which can be withheld. . . ."[23] So obstructing worked no harm, Symes thought, because any advantage "which the native might at the present stage of development obtain by getting credit for land would be of no value to him."[24]

The shackles on land as collateral indicate how much some administrators feared the potential of agricultural debt for creating a landless peasantry, their own land laws notwithstanding. Administrative supervision was necessary, Symes argued, to keep land free of a crushing burden of debt "which is so serious a problem all over East and Southern Europe."[25] Agricultural debt portended instability and a revolutionary climate, nightmares which others in Tanganyika had as the 1930s ended.[26]

Some Africans might have offered other types of property as collateral. These included dwellings and further capital improvements on the land, which they both possessed and owned in indigenous as well as colonial contexts. But administrative perceptions usually did not include them as potential collateral. Why most African dwellings were so excluded is related to the origins, evolution, and insidious impact of the convoluted legal distinction between hut and house. Though originating in tax legislation, this distinction and its justification narrowed collateral even more and may have discouraged many Africans from upgrading their dwellings.

RESTRICTED COLLATERAL (CONTINUED): HOUSES v. HUTS

The Municipal House Tax Ordinance empowered assessors to impose a rate not exceeding 15 percent on the net annual value of every house in any township. Net annual value was determined by the total rent a house might bring were it rented out for the year. In March 1930, Treasurer R. W. Taylor noted that this tax was imposed in certain townships and its rate varied from 0.5 percent to 5 percent. The central administration, moreover, got all the revenue.[27] From the outset, then, most administrators associated houses with townships. Although never a complete identification, this attitude worked against recognizing rural houses in the same terms. The Native Hut and Poll Tax Ordinance defined hut as "any hut, building, or structure of a description commonly used by natives as a dwelling." This definition is vague, circular, and perhaps too elastic. The major administrative problem was deciding when and if to call a hut a house, a task complicated by the overlapping of those two ordinances and concerns about stability. The guiding rule became quite simple: when in doubt, call it a hut.

Consider the tortuous emergence of that guideline. Government Notice No. 24 of 1930 stated that the huts of persons specified in Section 7 of the Hut and Poll Tax Ordinance (that might be houses) were exempt from the house tax. Section 7 exempted chiefs and headmen, among others, from the hut and poll tax, part of the social wage for serving the bureaucracy. In June 1933, the Acting Treasurer argued that Notice No. 24 was not necessary, because huts in townships were now liable to the hut tax. But, he said, certain "natives" eligible for exemption from the hut tax may "actually live" in houses taxable under the Municipal Tax Ordinance. There was, therefore, no basis for exemption from that ordinance; Notice No. 24 had only specified huts that "might" be houses, not actual houses. If Government desired exemptions for actual houses, it should amend the Municipal Tax Ordinance.[28] The question, as the Secretariat saw it, was: Should "natives" exempted from the hut tax under that ordinance be excused from the house tax if they really lived in a house and not a hut? The administration sidestepped this conundrum. Secretary Mitchell thought that because the dividing line between house and hut was not definite, one could not resolve the Treasurer's query.[29] And D. J. Jardine believed his question "of academic rather than practical interest" and concluded that "nothing should be done until a case arises."[30] Notice No. 24 was cancelled. But the Secretariat's evasion did not help the Treasury, which knew it had a practical problem.

In August 1933, that agency issued instructions for dealing with the question of ordinance overlap on some Africans. The Treasury recognized that some "natives" who could be granted a hut tax exemption lived in a house taxable under the House Ordinance. But H. R. Latreille, Chairman of the House Tax Commissioners, stipulated that where "a native, who is entitled to exemption under Section 7(1) of the Hut and Poll Tax Ordinance, is occupying a dwelling which is gradually being improved from a hut to a house, he should be treated as occupying a hut until it can be held without any shadow of doubt that the dwelling is a house."[31] Facing a rigorous standard rendered elusive by the absence of a practical

distinction between house and hut, one might never obtain certification
of a dwelling as a a house. Nor would those entitled to hut tax exemption
ever seek it, unless they wanted to pay the house tax.

But the possibility that some might lose their exemption concerned
Acting District Officer L. S. Guerning, Moshi, who reacted unfavorably
to that Treasury circular. Making the chiefs liable to house tax would hurt
a program of encouraging the Chagga to abandon their "old type, in-
sanitary, airless structures," because the chiefs, "who are setting the example," would feel aggrieved. He would try to maintain a comprehensive definition of hut, even though in Moshi "large numbers of natives
owned houses," including the chiefs. "In this district," Guerning noted,
paraphrasing the Hut and Poll Tax Ordinance, "houses are buildings
commonly used by natives as a dwelling and are therefore treated as
huts."[32]

Others had different reasons for preserving hut as the primary
"native" dwelling category. In November 1933, Secretary Mitchell, four
months after stressing the imprecise line between house and hut, observed that the correct approach seemed, at first sight, to charge "native
houses" of the better type the minimum rate of house tax. But, on closer
inspection, there were "serious political and some financial consequences
involved which we should avoid." What were these? ". . . It is the progressive, usually educated, coffee grower who builds himself a house instead of a hut. If we charge him house tax, we break almost the last remaining bond of duty between himself and his Chief and, incidentally,
deprive the Native Treasury of its share of his tax [hut and poll proceeds
went partly to Native Administration; house revenue all to central
bureaucracy]. This will be hotly resented by the Chiefs, and cannot fail to
encourage some at least of the house-holders in obstructive, if not subversive, courses."[33]

While administrators voiced fears of instability to justify maintaining hut as the overarching category, Africans faced tax differentials that
may have created disincentives for dwelling improvement. Secretary
Mitchell believed that an African who had improved his home and found
it recognized by the tax commissioners as a house would not pay an
amount of tax higher than the prevailing hut levy. In Bukoba and Moshi,
the two principal locations of the most concentrated and visible dwelling
improvement in Mitchell's opinion, the hut tax was twelve shillings,
which was the same as the "minimum rate of house tax." But his reasoning rests on a biased assumption about the net annual value of most
African homes and some incomplete arithmetic. "Since it is quite certain
that these houses in native rural areas would not fetch a rental of anything
like 12 pounds a year," Mitchell calculated, "the minimum house tax

would apply if they were assessed for house tax."[34] Under a 5 percent tax rate, an owner of a house with a net annual value of 12 pounds (240 shillings) would owe 12 shillings. But the law permitted rates up to 15 percent. So the Secretary considered only one actual rate, not the possible ceiling, and falsely stereotyped "native houses." There were disincentives. If one improved a dwelling too much, then the house might have a net annual value of more than 12 pounds. Even at 5 percent one would pay more than prevailing hut taxes in some locales. Better yet, keep one's home a hut and remove all possibility of a higher house tax.

So the elastic definition of hut and the disincentives present in those possible tax differentials worked, in the end, to deprive many Africans of an asset that should have qualified as legal collateral.[35] The inescapable fact was that, regardless of legal definition or practical variation, *hut* evoked in many minds images of smallness, shantiness, low-level living, and impermanence. The last of these was most devastating for anyone seeking a loan from a bank.

Many Africans disliked the entire apparatus of restrictive credit policy. When he was on tour in 1934, Gov. Harold MacMichael heard criticism from the Bukoba African Association, which he analyzed in his own post-interview notes. "They do not like the Restrictions of Credit Ordinance as applied to natives," the Governor observed. "I explained it was introduced for the protection of the natives as a whole, and that if someone wanted to borrow from an Indian for trade he could do so with D/C's permission [district commissioner]." Then in parentheses he added, "Apparently they had misunderstood the position. They also had amour propre in mind."[36]

The restrictive credit and collateral policies had harmful impacts not only on the self-respect or self-esteem of many Africans but also on their abilities and opportunities for engaging in exchange.

RESTRICTED CREDIT AND NARROWED COLLATERAL: IMPACT AND IMPLICATIONS

Government action almost froze African access to bank credit. Most bureaucrats, preoccupied with "native" credit as something small-time African traders got from small-scale Indian merchants and money-lenders, never considered bank loans as a serious form of credit for the "natives." But many Africans, including traders, might have used those loans to promote their own exchange activity had not the policy of restriction and its attendant perceptions of collateral affected banks operating in Tanganyika. One case from the official record shows how restricted access suffocated opportunity and perhaps it captures the thrust of other instances of deprivation not so preserved. On September 15, 1932, Mr. Issa bin Imangi, a Mwanza trader of apparently considerable means, wrote the Governor and asked that the restrictions imposed on him by credit legislation be relaxed. Imangi was upset; his bank had refused him credit allegedly "fearing the ordinance issued by H. E. [His Excellency the Governor] in 1923." Imangi presents the impact in such graphic terms that the reader should examine his testimony and recall that the revised 1931 ordinance exempted only trading contracts entered into by African traders, not other types of transactions.

Before we were dealing together our trade with Europeans and Indians, now the Europeans and Indian they are still dealing their trade, some they are putting their houses to the bank and they are getting credit from the Bank, but none of the Natives is allowed to get credit from the bank, for that reason I am begging help from the Government.

Also I have my two houses of Regestered one here at Mwanza and one at Nyanguge which I can put one to the Bank to get credit, therefore, Sir, I am begging help from his Excellency to help me to the Bank that I may put one of my house to get a credit of a few shillings from the Bank which can help me in my trading. . . .

. . . I am a trader, I know the work of trading very well, I am trying to put my house to the Bank the Bank refused fearing the Ordinance essued 1923. by the Government not to give credit to the Native traders, for that ordinance I am begging help from the Government to help me to get a credit from the Bank.[37]

On September 23, 1932, the Chief Secretary wrote the Provincial Commissioner, Lake, "Issa should approach D. O. [district officer], Mwanza, in matter of this nature."[38]

That is where the official record ends. The rejection apparently stood. Other evidence is needed to tell whether the ordinance itself was the primary reason for denial. Perhaps Imangi's houses would not have qualified as collateral even without credit legislation. Perhaps the bank saw something in Imangi's background that counseled caution. Maybe the request was excessive; "credit of a few shillings" is likely understated. Maybe the explanation lies in racial prejudice varnished with a rationale conveniently provided by government policy. In any event, Imangi's letter constitutes prima facie evidence supporting a contention that administrative action severely limited African access to bank credit, as either cause or ex post facto excuse.

Little wonder that evasion occurred. That it took place mainly in the least detectable theater—small-scale Afro-Indian commercial relations—

is significant. Some Africans contravened colonial law to obtain credit necessary for their livelihoods; but such actions further enmeshed them in a web of inequitable economic relationships. Even technically legal behavior strengthened this imbalance. Consider some implications of that 1931 exemption of trading contracts negotiated by license holders. Commenting on that revision, Secretary Jardine said, "If any non-native wishes to give credit to a native and to be in a position to recover his debts from the native, all that he will have to do apparently is to give the native 100/- to take out a Trading Licence and the 100/- would be presumably added to the recoverable debt."[39] Or give the "native" 20/- to purchase a special "native" trading license. "Non-natives" could thus buy recoverability by subsidizing Africans as trade licensees. How widespread was this practice? One can never obtain figures. Recipients of such largess were not likely to tell administrators where they got money to purchase a trading license. If they admitted assistance, they needed permission to contract that debt, unless "non-natives" regarded the money as a gift and did not add it to the recoverable debt. This action would have negated the rationale for the transaction in the first place. Indian financing of Africans as apparent traders in their own right was an important phenomenon. This behavior enlarged a group legally certifiable as traders who were in fact little more than financial extensions of the Indian merchants themselves. These people, in turn, regarded the licensees as "touts" or errand boys, if they really traded on a sustained basis at all.

Wherever Africans turned for credit beyond local ethnic sources, the vast majority found themselves shackled in one way or another. Sometimes the obstruction killed the kinds of opportunities for exchange that could have given individuals greater economic autonomy. Sometimes people found that to survive, they had to seize the dependent opportunities that restrictive credit policy fostered. In the end this action only intensified inequity.

The next chapter completes the three-part examination of exchange.

5

Organizing Official Markets:
Winners and Losers

T H R O U G H its organization of official markets, the Tanganyika administration had a significant impact on the location and mix of exchange activity and thereby affected both domestic and foreign economic relationships. To demonstrate this proposition, chapter 5 first considers the general strategy behind market organization and some contemporary reaction to it. It next takes up several issues associated with actual implementation, and then offers as case studies the few continuous clusters of examples available. Lastly, some implications of distorted market articulation for underdevelopment are summarized. The costs and benefits that official market organization imposed on different groups thus fashion a rough portrait of ''winners'' and ''losers.''

A STRATEGY OF CONCENTRATION:
THE TRADE-OFF BETWEEN MAXIMUM REVENUE
AND EFFICIENT CONTROL

Official market organization originated in the related necessities of revenue and stability. Market centers generated some revenue, but the administration assigned to them two more important fiscal functions. As arenas of compulsory cash transactions, they gave ''natives'' an opportunity to obtain the colonial coins that were used to pay hut and poll taxes. People trading in official centers might have their tax extracted on the spot, as local bureaucrats and their Native Authority surrogates tried to intersect market and collection cycles as much as possible. These two functions—cash diffusion and tax collection—were vital to the bureaucratic economy. To promote a maximum revenue yield in coin, administrators should have spread market centers throughout the territory. But this required some type of proximate supervision to ensure stability. So officers, their numbers and time already stretched, attempted to concentrate exchange activity in locations that seemed most suitable for efficient tax collection.

Some officials and others criticized this strategy of concentration based on administrative convenience. When the Legislative Council was in Committee on the Markets Bill of 1928, Mr. Ruggles-Brise, an unofficial European member, asserted, "It is suspected that the markets are used simply as a measure to secure the Hut and Poll Tax, and I do not think it should be so." Governor Cameron ruled this remark out of order. He commented, "I think the Honourable Member is speaking rather to the principle of the Bill than to its details. We are in Committee."[1] But the issue would not disappear. Six years later, at the second reading of the 1934 supply bill, M. P. Chitale, the articulate Indian spokesman, observed, "The marketing system naturally concentrates the trade in produce in a few selected areas, with the result that both producers and buyers have to transport goods a long way to reach that central place." "No doubt," he continued, "the Government thinks the system is good: from viewpoint of efficient tax collection. But tax collection is not only criteria of effective marketing system."[2]

Two critics took particular aim at constrained cash diffusion. On October 21, 1924, Mr. Wood, a cotton specialist working in Tanganyika for the Empire Cotton Growing Corporation, argued, ". . . from [its] effect on cotton production a case [can be] made for [the] outlying duka [shop] as a means of stimulating a desire on the part of the native for things which he can only obtain on payment of cash." For Wood and his metropolitan employer, diffusing cash incentives from dispersed shops might motivate people to produce more cash crops for export abroad by giving them a chance to buy something without a long safari to a central marketplace. But the cotton specialist acknowledged, "To the Administrative officer . . . the more these dukas are concentrated the more easy it is for him to control them, and this policy of concentration has been pushed further in some districts than others. . . ."[3] Director of Agriculture Harrison thought the twin emphases on concentration and collection detrimental. In December 1931, he stressed that some action was needed "to convey more *cash* to the native so that he can meet taxes, and exercise his own discretion as to whether he will spend or save money."[4] Should Government "alter the system of marketing to get cash to the growers, certain expenses [are] unavoidable and supervision of markets is important."[5]

But the Government would not alter its strategy of concentration for efficient tax collection. Administrators did, however, relax their insistence on standardization of form and permitted variations in how markets were run. The next section examines actual implementation and begins to consider the general fates of those who managed government markets, those who did or did not use official facilities, and those whose activities officers sought to suppress. The evidence here comes from scattered locations and is somewhat episodic. The section after implementation probes in more detail the impact of market policy on different people by presenting case studies.

OFFICIAL MARKET ORGANIZATION:
SOME GENERAL COSTS AND BENEFITS

In 1924 a conference of administrators in Dar es Salaam had resolved, ''. . . this meeting is in favour of the principle of trade centres and regards the hawker and pedlar as undesirable.'' While officers had clear objectives, their preferred means involved polar opposites even on paper. They said, ''. . . this meeting regards the system of sale of market dues to private persons for collection as highly undesirable, and supports rather the free market or the Government controlled market wherever possible.''[6] In practice, most official centers were neither completely free nor directly government controlled. Over them presided one of two managerial types—salaried market masters or lessees. Despite administrative opposition, the latter predominated, because salaried market masters were in short supply.

Officers continued to debate the merits of the two types, leaving no doubt about who besides themselves benefited most from official market organization. Taking only the issue of whether a ''leased approach''[7] was more susceptible to cheating than a market master system, Attorney General Drayton offered the following analysis in 1936. ''Consider that the lessee's profit consisted of the difference between what he bids at auction (for the right to keep all fees, stall rents, etc., for a certain period, usually one month) and what he collects in fees.'' Drayton argued that under this leasing or farming-out system cheating of ''natives'' was possible ''to a greater extent.'' Their complaints constituted the only check on the lessee, but since lessees gave no receipts, Drayton could not verify those allegations.[8]

Governor MacMichael disagreed and asserted that the experience of the Central Province Produce Markets proved the workability of the lessee system.[9] Argument really hinged not on practicality—MacMichael's focus—but on equitable functioning—Drayton's concern. H. Hignell, who had considerable administrative experience in the Central Province, wrote privately, ''The difficulty in securing reliable, efficient and honest market masters is the only sufficient reason for leasing markets.'' Then in a curious shift he contended that leasing was better, because the lessee "will usually see that there is no outrageous profiteering by a successful competitor."[10] The fatuous hope that one lessee would check the "outrageous profiteering" of another, if the markets were close enough for any competition to exist in the first place, made the real question not whether most lessees were making handsome profits but how great those were. (Without written receipts, the author could not specify magnitude.) That lessees everywhere benefited, however, is indisputable. No wonder that "reliable, efficient and honest" people willing to work for fixed salaries as market masters were hard to find.

The final consumers of goods from official market centers underwrote lessee benefits and paid much of the other overall costs of that organization in the end. The cheating of which Attorney General Drayton wrote allegedly characterized some relations between lessees and "natives" in particular markets. But sellers, in the absence of fixed prices, can transfer their costs, legitimate or otherwise, to buyers. And Tanganyika consumers were treated no differently from those elsewhere.

Two cases illustrate who really shouldered the ultimate burden, either through prices actually paid or in reduced consumption of expensive goods. The first concerns a revision of the Mwanza Market Bye-Laws in 1933, which attempted to reduce the previous fee schedule. In only three of thirteen categories, however, did transactions costs diminish. For example, the vendor of milk, not in a rented stall, still paid a one-cent toll on every bottle sold, but the seller of potatoes found that toll halved from two cents per kikapo to one cent. In the Secretariat, D. C. Campbell noted that the "existing scale of dues is considered too high, and the effect of these amendments will [be] to reduce the tolls on certain articles, with the object of reducing the cost of living for natives. . . ." If that were the objective, then the rationale for revising only three categories was not clear, because, as G. J. Partridge responded, "The changes are not extensive."[11]

The second case shows how market fees affected the conversion of steers into meat and comes from Kahama market records. There in the early 1930s a seller of steers on the hoof paid a toll of 2/– per animal, and a vendor of slaughtered steers paid 3/– for each carcass.[12] So when an African sold an animal to the butcher, he paid a two-shilling fee, and when that butcher displayed the dead animal for sale, he paid another three-shilling toll. This double extraction was by no means a local aberration. Philip Mitchell blamed "taxation" and "excessive" butchers' markups as two factors depressing the Tanganyika cattle trade and cited these figures to prove his argument. In 1933 beef on the hoof (250 pounds) at Dodoma, Singida, or Rwaya cost from 10/– to 30/– or from 4 to 12 cents a pound. Retail prices then averaged about 30 cents a pound, but were between 50 cents and 1/– in most towns, "where a great part of the meat is eaten."[13] Needless to say, the great majority of African consumers found those prices prohibitive.

But for those who sold goods either in- or out-market, the outcome was not so pellucid. Their specific cost-benefit configurations depended upon several factors. First consider the impact of official markets on prices. A strong conviction of reporting officers was that trading in government centers brought higher prices for most African sellers than did dealings out on the roads and in the bush with itinerant traders and touts, at least during the initial phase of market formation. This impression is acceptable, even though it comes from people who had a vested interest in showing that Africans gained from market organization and whose perceptions of transactions between itinerant traders and sellers were often biased.

Examine the following incomplete but available opinion sample. In 1925 the district officer, Malangali, reported his persistent efforts to get "natives to bring their saleable produce direct to the market and there reap the benefit of sales by auction instead of suffering from the one-sided transaction of pedlars, who derive large profits by obtaining these at a ridiculously low price from the natives in the bush and re-selling to Indian traders." He conceded, "Market dues are held up before the people by pedlars as a device on the part of a grasping government to deprive them of a portion of what is rightfully their entire and hard-earned due." But he was surprised "how slow the natives are to realise that, even minus fees, prices obtained in a market are nearly 50% better than those offered by pedlars."[14] The district officer, Kondoa-Irangi, noted that the "1932 institution of compulsory auction of produce at markets is an outstanding success . . . natives get a fair price and the traders make a legitimate profit as opposed to the previous system whereby the only substantial and invariable gainer was the quick-witted Itinerant trader."[15] And in 1938 the district officer, Shinyanga, related, "Reliable traders have estimated that nearly one half of the gum produced has been bought outside markets. Chiefs and headmen have been urged unceasingly to warn their people of the folly of this illicit system, for prices paid in the bush are by report scarcely one third of the market rates."[16]

How did price differentials fare as centers became more established? An answer lies, first, in how vulnerable different modes of market operation were to price manipulation and, second, in how willing and able buyers were to combine for that purpose. Official markets did employ several kinds of pricing mechanisms; their exact territorial mix over time is elusive. In the Lake Province, for instance, administrators were testing three arrangements in 1933. Each was aimed at securing a fair level of competition by letting prices function in a somewhat different way. The "Mwanza" system, which affected Mwanza, Maswa, and Musoma districts, used notice boards advertising prices that every market stall holder agreed to pay for produce offered to him. In Kwimba district auction markets prevailed, while Shinyanga district allowed sales for cash at produce merchants' shops with prices indirectly controlled by a central auction market.[17]

How much, if at all, each mode promoted fair competition in the Lake Province is not apparent. But evidence from other locations suggests that the auction market and its variations were especially open to manipulation. One southern example shows that even the central administration admitted that fact. In 1931 the district officer recommended sanctioning a market at Mbalizi in the Mbeya area. Foodstuffs would be auctioned there. The Secretariat refused this request, because "the bye-laws for which approval is sought have not been made by a Native Authority but by the D. O. at the instance of the Lupa miners." The refusal noted, "There is no evidence that it is desired by the Native Authorities." Further, "It will affect adversely natives from the neighbouring District of Tukuyu."[18] Had a food auction market been approved, the Lupa miners would have formed a ring to buy produce at the lowest possible price. In the aborted Mbalizi case, a ring would have been an immediate possibility. In other instances there was a time lag between market initiation and buyer mobilization. But the common result of collusion on any timetable was depressed prices, which narrowed market-favorable differentials and may have eliminated them altogether, depending on location.

African producers did confront a constellation of potential benefits and liabilities in deciding whether to use official centers. Benefits included possibly higher prices, the necessity and desirability of obtaining government money, and the opportunity in some areas to purchase a greater variety of consumer goods. The negative side included the actual and opportunity costs of transporting goods to market and making the return trip. Above all, using a government market considerably reduced the chances of evading the hut and poll tax collectors, as the "cash nexus" often became the "cash net." And while those costs were ever present, there was no guarantee of a better price or a greater variety of consumer goods. In fact, market prices might change during the trip there, perhaps as a result of local supply and demand fluctuations or from buyer manipulation, which made the calculation of benefits all the more risky. There is no census, of course, listing who used and who avoided which government centers. Based on what official market organization meant for many Tanganyikans, the final part of this section shows how market policy affected mobile traders and their activities, specific targets of administrative intervention.

Many officers were convinced that a strategy of concentration, in some cases bolstered by abolishing pedlars' licenses, reduced itinerant trading and led to an increase in the number of stationary shops. What happened to the traders themselves is not always clear. The district officer, Tabora, noted one startling effect of eliminating pedlars' licenses in the mid-1920s, ". . . there are already 910 shops in the Province being run by natives."[19] And the same action in Shinyanga district "has increased Native shops from 21 in 1924 to 119 in 1925," the local officer reported. Since 95 percent of those pedlars were "aliens," he continued, "little or no hardship was imposed on the local natives." In fact, "the Chiefs and natives welcome the abolition of these promiscuous traders . . . their method of business was to intercept the producers on their way to established centres."[20] District Officer W. S. G. Barnes, Kondoa-Irangi, attributed the declining numbers of itinerant traders there, from 127 to 108 between 1928 and 1929, to "the additional markets which have been established and the opening up of the new trade centres." He elaborated, "The market and trading-centre policy has had the effect of closing numbers of small native shops scattered in odd corners of the district and of materially reducing the number of itinerant traders. The villager is realising that he can obtain a better bargain for the grain he wishes to sell or the articles he wishes to buy, by attending a trade centre where competition exists."[21]

In the Tabora and Shinyanga cases, some of the Indians who lost their pedlars' licenses may have set up African employees in stationary shops. This intuition rests on the Tabora officer's qualification that "many of these [910 "native" shopkeepers], although they have taken out licenses in their own names, are still employees of Indian merchants. . . ."[22] In the Kondoa-Irangi example what those people who ceased itinerant trading did is not clear; some might themselves have become stationary traders or sponsored other merchants. Nor is there any way to know how many "native" shopkeepers in the district relocated in official centers. Although the fate of individual mobile traders is sometimes difficult to determine, the impact of administrative intervention in many locations is straightforward. A diverse menu of transactions options for much of the territory's economic activity was shortened and somewhat standardized.

Not everyone accepted this compression with resignation, as the reactions of some demobilized itinerant traders indicate. In fact, the regulated tried, with mixed results, to stay one step ahead of the regulators. The next section develops that theme and further illuminates the impact of market policy on people's actual and potential economic relationships.

CASE STUDIES FROM THE CENTRAL AND WESTERN AREAS

The richest series of recorded, surviving, and available examples come from central and western sites, especially Dodoma district in the Central Province.

In the Dodoma district the initial administrative approach was vigorous consolidation. Before 1926, as District Officer A. V. Hartnoll reported, all trading in export produce was confined to four townships: Dodoma, Bahi, Kikombo, and Gulwe. He noted, "The policy has been to squeeze out economically the outlying dukas and make all traders conduct a cash business in properly surveyed townships." What Hartnoll termed an incomplete restoration of "free trade" ensued after promulgation of the 1925 Secretariat Circular on "Markets and Trade."[23] Government licensed merchants "to trade freely where they liked,"[24] established various trading centers, and invited business people to bid for sites in those locations. The offer was spurned. "The sales were a failure," because who wanted "to be hampered with a 33 years' lease, containing provisions for building substantial shops?" Establishing trading centers and introducing site leases conflicted with local commercial patterns, as merchants preferred to "rent Gogo mud huts and move about from place to place in search of business." But administrative law converted economic preference into criminal vulnerability. The Provincial Commissioner ruled in late 1926 that "it was illegal for these Indians to rent communal land" and tried to stop such activity.[25]

Officers also decided that efficient centralization, as distinct from mere consolidation, required establishment of more trade centers outside townships. Some began functioning in 1927; "each . . . has its little market and all produce brought within a radius of one mile from the market centre must be sold by auction on the market square"; dues were 5 percent. But as administrators pursued greater regulation of both town and country, the merchants became more mobile. There was "a great rise in the number of motor vehicles owned by merchants," usually Chevrolet one-ton lorries, which "traders are using more and more for the transport of produce to the railway." Merchants thus were motorized itinerant traders; "many traders preferred to establish themselves outside these centers in their motor lorries, and supplied with itinerant traders licenses, buy the produce, thereby saving the market dues."

The truck was not the only obstacle to official organization; there were at least three more. For example, supervising scattered markets was not easy; Native Authorities "are still in an illiterate infancy."[26] In addition, auctioning the markets proved cumbersome at Dodoma and Mpwapwa because that "played into the hands of Indian trade rings. . . ." And "it has been difficult to find local residents who are prepared to take on the markets for any length of time."[27]

One obstruction the administration did eliminate. This action came in a 1927 incident that demonstrates conflicts not only between in- and out-market trading but also within the business community itself. A certain Ali Remtulla outbid all rivals for the lease of Kikombo market and, in accordance with standard operating procedure, he won it. According to Provincial Commissioner Henry Hignell, his competitors then took out trading licenses "giving vague or no details as to the site of their proposed branch businesses" and sat down on every road to Kikombo. "By telling the peasants that by selling to them they escaped market dues they stifled the central market." Then the traders erred; they became stationary in an illegal fashion. "We could do nothing until they had snugly ensconced themselves in various well placed native *tembes* [flat-roofed houses]. Under the Land Amendment Ordinance we could then deal with them for being in improper possession of public land," he added. And the Governor himself tightened another screw, "Every native owner or trader must hold a right of occupancy to the land on which non-native business premises are situated."[28] Hignell concluded, ". . . to avoid this real risk of having every tribal authority in the pocket of the local traders, rights of occupancy should be recommended at present for sites in well defined market centres."[29] The administration won this round.

But organization proceeded slowly in Dodoma district. Officer Wilkins reported in 1928, ". . . the local traders are still averse to making use of recognised markets and revenue has suffered accordingly."[30] Although the number of trading centers increased from thirteen to thirty during 1928, the majority of these were not an unqualified success. Locating there meant four things for traders: first, cash payments for produce bought by auction; second, increased purchase prices owing to competition; third, payment of ground rent for a plot; and, fourth, payment of a house tax on the erected building.[31] Put another way, buyers in official centers faced at least four possible transactions costs. The second might have become a seller's benefit, but the others helped the administration.

Some Indian traders continued to resist. The way Wilkins portrayed their actions shows how market organization also contributed to the growth of dependency for African traders. He said the Indians tried "many ways of avoiding these payments, firstly, by trading in Gogo tembes and then by licensing Native Traders with a 20/- Shs. Licence and supplying them with goods, in some cases to a value of 1000/- Shillings, but in such a way that no conviction could be obtained from breach of regulations under the Trades Licensing Ordinance. They also made use of the Pedlars Licence in conjunction with one or more motor lorries, establishing their own markets on roads leading to townships and existing Trading Markets or under trees out in the bush."[32] These tactics were somewhat successful. Trade in recognized centers declined, as demonstrated by falling market revenue (1925: Shs. 86,971; 1926:61,159; 1927:48,727; and 1928:26,998).

The bureaucracy responded with greater regulation, but these measures were only partially effective. Officer Wilkins insisted that the "trading centres with their markets" be protected and believed the outlook happier under Ordinance No. 37 of 1928. He claimed the ordinance prohibited the sale of goods in an area within three miles from the boundaries of any market. This buffer zone produced mixed results. It reduced some patent evasions in Dodoma but pushed the zone of "illegal" transactions outward, as "the use of a pedlars licence with one or more motor lorries is still a very severe stumbling block to progress in this direction."[33]

In the early 1930s administrators evidently reverted to the pre-1926 policy of excessive consolidation for the central area. Provincial Commissioner Hignell observed in 1932 that "sales of native produce [were] confined to produce markets." He called this move a first step in the complete reconstruction of the "old market system" and argued that it had already stimulated a threefold increase in groundnuts production from 1931. In the midst of this maneuvering some Africans, according to Hignell, had "asked that central markets—which set the price for all other markets—should be controlled by Government employees so that they could know what prices to expect anywhere by making allowance for transport."[34] Whether they wanted efficient central price fixing or an honest management that let supply and demand forces have full play is not clear. But their rejection of leased central markets was unmistakable. It anticipated and perhaps even motivated Attorney General Drayton's more general critique cited earlier in this chapter.

Examples from western Tanganyika illuminate the struggle between the regulators and regulated, the impact of a reduced exchange menu on economic opportunity, and the details on why the administration tolerated an uneconomic level of petty trading. Examine first another installment in Government v. itinerant traders. In 1932 Provincial Commissioner Richards, Lake Province, quarreled with the Arab Association over issuance of itinerant traders' licenses. This group claimed that many traders had to pay 50/– for an itinerant license that otherwise cost 20/–; in fact, what they bought was a retail trade license (excluding importation). Richards admitted he had restricted itinerant issuance, because merchants used them as a "cloak to the carrying on of a business which should be licenced under T. L. O. [Trades Licensing Ordinance] . . . these activities cost a considerable loss of revenue to Government." This evasive cloak was extensive. He reported that some itinerant traders, both "native" and "non-native," sit on the side of a road just outside a trading settlement and intercept "natives" carrying produce to the center for sale. At the same time licensed shopkeepers employ "natives," take out itinerant trading licenses for them, and these "sit side by side" with the first group and compete in "touting" for business.

What especially galled Richards was a recent development. "And now Indians and others with I.T. licences open temporary stalls at places not necessarily in the vicinity of trading settlements and attend there daily travelling to and fro by lorry for trading," he said. They paid no land rent nor house tax; "as soon as it is known that an Administrative Officer is in the vicinity the traders quickly disperse and no evidence is obtainable that they were not legitimately acting as itinerant traders." Richards asserted that most of the "legitimate trading community" was "anxious that itinerant trading should be done away with" and that "no hardship" would befall "genuine native traders who can always take out a native trading licence at the same rate of 20/–."[35] The Chief Secretary informed Richards that his general refusal to grant itinerant licenses was *ultra vires*, although "specific unexplained refusals" were "possible."[36]

Reducing the numbers of itinerant traders, selectively or collectively, decreased transactions options and constricted economic opportunity. If there were an oversupply of mobile traders in an area, diminution might not create harm. But in some districts demand for mobile trading services equalled or exceeded available supply, and administrative harassment generated problems. The experience of the Musoma district in the mid-1920s is one example. The district officer there noted, "Collection of the economic crop was somewhat difficult owing to the curtailment of native hawkers to such as were trading for their personal gain on the establishment of Trading Settlements. The native in the past waited for the native hawker to come to him in order to purchase his stock and was very loath to take his supply to the Trading Settlements."[37] Roving hawkers eliminated sellers' costs of using official centers and, whether or not they overcharged for their services by paying too low purchase prices, constituted a vital part of the Musoma exchange process.

Several officers accepted the necessity for some mobile trading and defined what they considered the most desirable supply mix of different kinds of traders. For District Officer A. W. M. Griffith, Bukoba, the hierarchy of preference was clear: '' . . . the native trader who pays for his goods in cash and is beginning to purchase his stock direct from the local wholesalers may become a valuable asset but it will take time. The Indian or Arab trader in the bush also consitutes a valuable stimulus to trade but the majority of small bazaar traders in Bukoba and Kamachumu serve no economic purpose and prejudice fair competition by their commercial immorality.''[38]

Whatever an officer's preferences, he usually yielded to the exigencies of stability. In chapter 3, for example, the Acting Provincial Commissioner, Lake, attacked a proposal to abolish the special "native" trading license on the grounds that such action would foster "grave discontent" and might hasten the "formation of co-operative societies." His criticism came in 1936. Officers in that area had not always been so tolerant of the large numbers of African traders of various types. Their earlier policies and the trade-off decision that prompted relaxation are the subjects of the next vignette, drawn from the Bukoba experience.

By all accounts the number of African trade licensees in that district exceeded what the volume of trade required, especially during the 1920s. In 1925, for instance, about 7,000 people held pedlars' licenses. Local officers analyzed and, at the outset, tried to contain this uneconomic expansion. They cancelled the exemption from performing compulsory service for the licensee's chief, which holding a trade document conferred. Numbers dipped but continued high and bothersome. In 1925 Senior Commissioner Brett argued that two financial factors—the "low cost of the license" and "occasionally very high and quick profits"— sustained the level of licensing. But he emphasized another factor, at once a political benefit for traders and a problem for bureaucrats, ''. . . the unsatisfactory feature presented by the petty [African] traders lies in their tendency to organise themselves as an association.'' They "have recognised leaders in each village and the latter have sometimes endeavoured to act independently of the native authorities and have claimed a special recognition in administrative matters." Brett thought further organization unlikely, although he recommended without result that more activity should be met with "a substantial increase in the fee charged for the licence in order to reduce the numbers.''[39]

Trader organization continued as something of a shadow government beside Native Administration, but the special license fee was not increased. Most administrators in the 1930s realized that cooperatives would bring them more problems than traders' societies. Two factors, especially, did not calm the administration: co-ops had greater potential for coherent, lasting, political and economic organization; and they upset Indian associations. The Bukoba Indian community, in particular, expressed grave dissatisfaction over rumors of impending cooperative organization in the mid-1930s. True to its best interests, the group argued that "fierce" competition would assure African producers of the "best possible price."[40] Far better, then, to put up with the lesser of destabilizing threats, although this approach perpetuated as its short- and long-term economic costs a bloated service component in some areas.

DISTORTED INTERNAL MARKET ARTICULATION AS ONE
FORM OF UNDERDEVELOPMENT

While the benefits and harms of official market organization varied depending on time, location, and group, its general and consistent effect was to distort internal market articulation. This chapter emphasized distortions affecting locations of exchange, supply mix of traders, and menus of available transactions options. These all resulted because most administrators pursued a market deepening (concentration) based more on narrow financial criteria than on broader economic considerations and campaigned against general market widening (diffusion). Officials refused to devise a pattern of structures that would have matched the territory's demographic and economic contours. They also endeavored to dismantle many of the dispersed intermediate links they found and installed revenue efficiency as the primary desideratum in market location. This manipulation of past market articulation fostered a kind of underdevelopment that primarily benefited the bureaucracy. In fact, markets were more extensions of the administration than energizers of exchange or economic expansion.

This particular mode of market organization did not enhance the territory's capacity to produce cash crops for export or to absorb more imports of consumer goods. Limiting cash diffusion by concentrating shops did, as cotton specialist Wood noted earlier, skew both the distribution of cash and the supply of consumer items. Reducing transactions options likely decreased the volume of trade in some areas. However, many officers accepted what District Officer W. S. G. Barnes had written about Kondoa-Irangi: the added business done by each shop in established trading centers "more than made up for the loss of trade formerly handled by the smallest type of shopkeeper and the itinerant trader."[41] While the absence of out-market records makes the latter issue moot, there is no doubt that maldeveloped market organization constrained the territory's international relationships. Some may now regard this as a blessing. But the key domestic damage was the suppression in many places of a grass-roots, horizontal economic integration that would have provided the greatest benefits for the greatest number of Tanganyikans.

Ironically, even one of the administration's most cherished inter-war programs, the "plant-more-crops" campaign, encountered the constraints of skewed cash and consumer commodity distribution. But bureaucrats were not daunted. The next three chapters examine administrative intervention in agriculture, each with a different emphasis.

6

Manipulating Agriculture:
The "Plant-More-Crops" Campaign

INITIATED in the early 1930s and revised later, the "plant-more-crops" campaign represented the most concerted endeavor to fashion a territorial agricultural policy during the inter-war period. Throughout the decade this program aimed at general objectives based on the administration's calculus of maximization and minimization. In its evolving design, its more refined implementation, and cumulating local effects, one can see perhaps the most coherent case study of the bureaucratic economy at work.

To suggest what the rather vague phrase "policy evolution" meant for both administrators and the administered, this chapter tracks the campaign through the 1930s, following its rubrics of objectives, design, implementation, and impact. It illustrates, where possible, how the operation of the campaign conflicted with what unofficials and even some officials thought desirable. Some implications of the campaign for an internal administrative organization of underdevelopment are also considered.

PHASE ONE: PUSHING THE "NATIVES" TO PRODUCE MORE EXPORT CROPS

In the 1920s many bureaucrats had emphasized the crucial connection between increased cash crop production for export and revenue yields. Put simply, those crops bolstered both direct and indirect tax returns. Receiving the bureaucracy's cash for their output enabled Tanganyikans to pay hut and poll taxes in the preferred remitting medium. And as these crops moved through the market network, indirect taxes generated more revenue. Few officers expressed that relationship more concisely than did Provincial Commissioner Henry Hignell writing his semiannual report on the Central Province in June 1928: "To help the revenue position," he exhorted, "we must get every nut we can out of the province."[1]

The impact of the Great Depression upon Tanganyika transformed that conviction into a territorial program with direction to come from the center. Revenue from such key levies as hut and poll taxes and import duties sagged in the early 1930s, a delayed but inescapable confirmation of contracting economic activity in both international and domestic spheres. The Tanganyika administration responded to financial decline with a consistency that was altogether single-minded. The Territory had to lean on its agricultural strength to produce more crops for export, regardless of what the international demands for particular commodities were at the time.

In 1932 Gov. Stuart Symes noted that some regarded this behavior as eccentric. Production was stressed "at a time when economists suggest that overproduction is a prime factor in the world's stress and that it is consumption and purchasing power that require stimulation . . . "[2] So began the first phase of the "plant-more-crops" campaign, which progressed erratically in the early 1930s under uneven enthusiasm and direction. Then it faded with a few staccato bursts of energy in the mid-1930s, only to be revived with greater coherence and purpose in 1938.

Phase one concentrated on "native" or "peasant" agriculture for more specific reasons of revenue maximization. In 1930 R. W. Taylor, then Treasurer, wrote the Chief Secretary and asserted that "increased production is the ideal. It does not matter whether it is Native or non-Native so long as the goods are produced."

Governor Cameron, however, disagreed in a crucial marginal note: "Not quite. The native . . . spends all his profits in the country."[3] Cameron clearly realized that the bureaucracy gained to the extent that returns from production were internalized within the territory. His perception became a central premise of the first phase, which called on "natives" to produce more of all their crops except coffee. (Because of usually higher monetary returns per unit of labor input, coffee-growing needed not encouragement but control, an endeavor discussed in chapter 8.)

If the gross twin objectives of the campaign were clear—plant more crops to generate more revenue—the precise design was not. There were several sources of ambiguity. The first consisted of inexact microeconomic targets. Tanganyika's Department of Agriculture, the primary technical agency pushing phase one, never specified what might be feasible increments in production for particular crops in definite locations, although it did propose aggregate territorial goals. Growers thus faced unrefined demands to plant more and more in the shortest possible time.

The second source of ambiguity came from the forms that those demands took. In his diary entry for November 26, 1932, Secretary of Native Affairs Philip E. Mitchell alluded to the "plant-more-crops" campaign. He referred to "an absurd letter from Wakefield [in the Agriculture Department] suggesting that every European official in the Provinces should be turned loose on the unhappy natives to harass them to plant more crops."[4] In their public statements officials used more muted language; "supervision," "encouragement," and "exhortation" replaced harassment.

Whatever the forum or choice of words, one basic fact was clear. Administrative pressure, transmitted by combinations of impersonal ordinances, personal directives, and Native Court enforcement, generated demands to produce more. But in phase one the central bureaucracy never defined the precise degree of pressure officers might exert. This heightened the already present possibility that local growers would hear conflicting administrative voices.

A third source of ambiguity in design came from official approaches to market forces such as prices. From an administrative standpoint, prices should function as fair rewards for those long hours of labor counseled by the hard work ethic. And these rewards should not fluctuate too much. Dislike of price fluctuations reflected that general preoccupation with stability in every dimension. It gained intensity when officers observed the effects of declining prices on producers' planting decisions. Of their many recorded statements on relations between prices and output, two examples illustrate the prevailing convictions of most bureaucrats.

In 1928 W. F. Page, district officer for Kwimba, remarked on some vacillations in prices for "native" output. "This fluctuation," he explained, "is difficult for the native to understand and is apt to leave him with the impression, judging by the frequent questions asked, that he is not getting a fair deal from the buyers. It understandably militates somewhat against larger production."[5]

The Department of Agriculture in its 1931 report analyzed some more ominous consequences of decreased production for the territory and proposed the familiar administrative solution: "The African remembers only the good times, and whenever a low price obtains, he cuts down or ceases production. He thus becomes incapable of carrying out the lowest functions and obligations that should be expected of a citizen of any state; his buying capacity is so lowered, especially in areas of annual cash crops, that a general stagnation of trade results, adding further to the general depression. The remedy here lies in greater production."[6]

If the clear remedy was greater production, a staggering problem became how to make prices fair and rewards stable. To begin with, there were formidable difficulties in defining fairness and stability. What criteria should determine a fair price or return for each agent and agency in the economic process has provoked debate for centuries. Put simply, which contributors should get what? And on what basis? And one still had to translate guidelines into numbers, a most intractable practical problem. Tanganyikan bureaucrats confronted all these problems concerning fairness and also faced an acute translation question in relation to stability. At what point do price changes become destabilizing fluctuations for particular crops? Defining acceptable zones of price movement was as vexing as matching constructs of fairness with numbers.

By their inadequate solutions, central administrators acknowledged the magnitude of those problems and created a third source of ambiguity for local growers. Some prices were the objects of more intense administrative manipulation than others. Attempting to regulate local cotton prices in the 1930s was the most significant intervention of that sort. This endeavor is analyzed in the next chapter on cotton regulation but is mentioned here to emphasize the inconsistency in overall price design.

The Tanganyika bureaucracy would reject inconsistency for selective manipulation. But many growers no doubt wondered why other market forces working on other crop prices, whatever those forces really masked, did not receive as much attention. Were some market forces more beneficial or detrimental than others? Why stable rewards only for the cotton industry? Would concerted price regulation extend to other crops and, if so, when? These questions served mainly to define, not eliminate, another source of ambiguity.

A final and perhaps most critical origin of ambiguity resided in the sometimes contradictory courses of action suggested by prices and dictated by pressures. When bureaucrats urged growers to produce more of a crop that brought less, their financial rationale collided with a near universal logic of economic efficiency. According to this logic, one can construe price declines as signals of oversupply or as effects of some market manipulation, rigidity, or imperfection adverse to grower welfare. However African farmers really analyzed the reasons for price reductions, their decisions to decrease production seem wholly consistent with this basic economic logic. What the administration could not regulate with structures it tried to override with propaganada: growers should produce more for the good of the territory. The revenue that increased output brought might finance more ''native'' social services. Whatever the prevailing price, growers were better off planting something than nothing.

These ambiguities in design do not altogether explain the problems encountered in implementation. Of course, some officers wondered how hard they could push local growers. In some cases, this led to little or no administrative pressure; in others, an erratic application of official pressure. But a great majority used the full arsenal of persuasive techniques, including Native Court sanctions for personal failure to comply with government-sponsored directives. Local officers sometimes questioned whether the centrally administered cotton price was fair. Some even refused to encourage cotton planting until they adjudged the price equitable for growers. But most tried to implement the campaign's major objectives with a minimum of quibbling.

In fact, it was this single-minded concentration on "native" production that created more irritating practical problems for the administration. Some "non-native," unofficial interests complained that the campaign was harming their enterprises by reducing their labor supply. These people argued that in some locations administrative pressure kept Africans at home farming who otherwise would have worked for them. Several protests reached the Colonial Office in due course where they evoked a somewhat different analysis of the origins of alleged reduction in labor supply.

Mr. F. Lee noted in 1937, "There have already been broad hints, both from the Mining and from the Sisal industries, that the activities of the Agriculture Department, in stimulating native production should be restrained, so that natives will not be tempted to stay at home and grow crops rather than go to work for non-native enterprise." But Lee hoped "that the Tanganyika Government will not accede" because the "sisal industry [was] not trying to help itself get labour by increasing wages, despite the improvement in the price of sisal."[7]

However, Gov. Harold MacMichael was moving to reduce friction by working out a modus vivendi with representatives of the sisal industry. Sometime in the mid-1930s he and the Tanganyika Sisal Growers Association arrived at a gentlemen's agreement that put a portion of Tanga Province off limits for government propaganda designed to stimulate "native" cotton production.[8] It is hard to estimate who gained more. The relaxation of administrative pressure in that restricted area presumably made labor recruiting less difficult. Whether or not the supply of labor increased because of that action is hard to say. Government's gains seemed more distinct. MacMichael had succeeded in excluding the Luengera valley, a prime cotton-growing region, from the area of no propaganda, and pressure there continued unrelenting.

This dispute over labor supply introduces the more general question of the campaign's overall impact in phase one. Director of Agriculture E. Harrison claimed success because by 1935 the territory had reached the quantitative production goals that he advocated. Although one cannot measure the precise extent to which the campaign itself was responsible for those results, the more intense pressure did encourage increased production. But success for the bureaucracy in those gross quantitative terms was significantly harmful to the people and resources of Tanganyika in terms of major distortions in factor allocation and in the language of economic communication.

Distorted factor allocation means that at least one of the basic economic factors of production—land, labor, capital, and entrepreneurial ability—was so used as to violate some canon of efficiency or optimization. Identifying misuse and appraising its significance depend, of course, on whose standards are employed. And specifying extent requires a statistical minimum of data on such items as productivity, wages, and prices. For identification, this chapter relies partly on the testimony of contemporary witnesses who argued from their own perceptions of economic common sense. Because information on input productivity has proved elusive, the precise degrees of distortion cannot be specified. The reader must accept a prima facie case based on impression and logic.

The most widespread distortions occurred in land and labor allocation. Two particular misuses stand out: land overuse and an overallocation of African labor towards export production.

Consider land abuse first. No one put an indictment more pungently than did the man who became Chief Engineer of the Tanganyika Railway administration in 1928. In his diary entry for May 9, 1935, C. Gillman commented at length on the ''plant-more-crops'' campaign:

As so often before, I was meditating and preaching again the ''Plant more crops policy,'' our Director of Agriculture's pet, accepted blindly and fostered by Government. To my mind, and of course to everybody's mind (as long as that mind is exercised!) Agricultural Production is based on *Land plus Labour* and one simply can not merely increase the latter and leave out of consideration the increased stress on the former! But that is exactly what the ''Plant more crops and destroy your Land Policy'' does. I am not led by sentimentality towards the native and I fully agree with the Harrisons and Maxwells and Symeses that more labour will not do any harm to the native peasant. But I insist that this extra labour should be employed for something more lasting and more solid than a temporary increase of Revenue through taxation and railway traffic at the cost of an irretrievable deteriorating of soil and water. The snag is, of course, the labour used in this right direction, i.e. towards husbanding the soil instead of mining for increased crops, would most likely render the crops unable to compete at this distance from the world's markets, and would thereby expose too glaringly for the egotistical ''Administrators'' and merchants the fallacy of Africa's untold and dormant potentialities; a phrase which, as long as it is believed in, helps admirably to fill fiscal and commercial coffers at the expense of the Land and of those future generations who will have to depend on it. And that's that! And I should like to meet anyone who can detect the slightest flaw in my argument.[9]

The snag resides not in the logic of his argument, which is correct, if overstated, but in verification. Existing written records do not contain information sufficient to determine the varieties of soil deterioration, the extent to which they did occur, and the way any overuse compelled by the campaign contributed to that abuse. Nonetheless, the problem of land overuse was significant. More criticisms of abuse, from both insiders and outsiders, continued to assail the administration throughout the 1930s.

Administrative pressure distorted the allocation of African labor but not usually in the way those alien enterprises alleged. The campaign did influence some Tanganyikans to farm who might have worked for others. But one cannot argue that if there had been no pressure, those people would then have so labored. Too many factors challenge that inference. These include how those potential workers estimated their demands for official money and how they assessed the wage schedules, working conditions, and modes of direct tax collection associated with different alien enterprises (see chapter 2). What their decisions would have been with little or no pressure is impossible to fathom. In any event, the central fact is that what administrative diversion did occur probably was not a real distortion in most cases. Without evidence on the comparative productivity of African labor in all its uses, this statement is mere conjecture. But alien enterprise did not, in general, pay African workers in relation to their contributions. Even if one concedes employer complaints about low worker productivity, wage scales were in most cases exceedingly low. So "natives" farming by themselves under administrative supervision may have yielded, depending on commodity and price, returns that diverged less from real physical product. This outcome represented a more efficient allocation of labor between those two alternative uses.

This speculation assumes that labor so invested in the production of cash crops for export did not detract from the performance of other tasks imposed by local agrarian cycles. In fact, administrative pressure led many Tanganyikans to overemphasize export crop production and, in consequence, to neglect in varying degrees such domestic demands as those for food crops of different kinds. Written evidence demonstrating this distortion in labor allocation is largely circumstantial. The Bukoba incident of 1928–1929 involved intense pressure to plant cotton, with consequent local food scarcities, and allegations of famine-related deaths. It illustrated one horrible outcome of overallocation.[10] To what extent this episode prefigured what actually happened in the 1930s is hard to say. But there is circumstantial evidence that indirectly establishes the impact of export pressure on food production for domestic consumption. Local officers more often invoked sections of colonial legislation that required every household to plant foodstuffs sufficient for its own needs. In some cases actual or anticipated food shortages from natural causes prompted such action. But the majority of invocations likely confirm the campaign's distorting impact on labor allocation. And all acts of compulsion further entrenched the bureaucratic incubus in agriculture.

Phase one wrought its second major set of distortions on the language of economic communication. These distortions, which consisted of confusions in concepts and symbols more than physical misallocation, emerged from the administration's mixing markets of prices with markets of pressures. In fairness, some bureaucrats did not analyze the results of their actions in that way. Director of Agriculture E. Harrison, for example, defended the campaign in 1934 and interwove the theme of territorial stability with that of the bureaucracy's mission in economic education. "Despite the criticisms of the policy of increasing production," he asserted, "there is no question of its utility and, as a direct result, there is much more faith in the stability of the territory. It is important too that groups of people who had no idea of anything but a life of bare subsistence should be encouraged to do something more than that. . . ."[11] In 1935 A. J. Wakefield, then acting Director of Agriculture, made these points more concisely: ". . . the 'plant-more-crops' campaign has proved to have had a considerable educative value in addition to its material and economic effect."[12] But this mission in economic education, which aimed to revise what bureaucrats thought was indigenous acceptance of a low standard of living, distorted far more than it clarified, partly as a result of those ambiguities in the campaign's design.

Inexact microeconomic production targets created at least two distortions, but it should first be noted how they destabilized decision making by intensifying the uncertainties always associated with agriculture. This uncertain environment did not facilitate economic re-education but served as background against which those distortions may seem more harmful. The first concerns the notion of economic surplus. Scholars often argue the meaning and applicability of this concept in different contexts. In this case the government distorted Harrison's implied definition of surplus in implementing the campaign. To encourage production beyond bare subsistence, itself a moot concept, presumably means that the notion of surplus must function as an incentive in some sense. That is, producers must recapture some benefits from generating surplus in ways they deem meaningful and equitable, whatever the categories and standards of assessment. But the campaign so identified surplus with distant beneficiaries (the territory), vague promises (higher funding for "native" social services), and questionable axioms (hard work for its own sake) that it became almost synonymous with extraction and expropriation.

In considering production only, those targets distorted in a second way—by downplaying the importance farmers should attach to feasible distribution in their planting decisions. Without adequate storage facilities, only the eccentric would produce with little concern for immediate marketing possibilities. But the campaign encouraged shortsighted behavior. Leading bureaucrats were especially myopic. In 1935 A. J. Wakefield argued, "Merely because the science of production has temporarily out-stripped the organization of distribution, this can hardly be taken as a reason why the lower standard should be adopted. . . ."[13] He presumed an automatic relationship between increasing production and a rising material standard of living upon which the administration's economic education mission so precariously rested.

How the bureaucracy used its own language in the campaign resulted in more distortion. The victims were certain words and phrases and, indirectly, those who spoke or wrote them unaware of their history of abuse. The author has elsewhere analyzed language manipulation in colonial Tanganyika.[14] There the impact of the dissolving differences among a cluster of words—encouragement, exhortation, wish, order, and command—upon government's capacity to direct economic activity with any sense of distinct priority was assessed. He also showed how the bureaucracy's artificial agronomic nomenclature distorted activity when it divided crops into two major categories. "Food crops" designated output produced and consumed locally. Commodities grown at home but shipped abroad and sold for cash had such interchangeable names as "export," "cash," or "economic" crops. This gross distinction, relaxed only when a few officers decided some crops fit in both groups, partitioned activity in a harmful way, as if wider distribution of food crops within the territory was not economic.

The final distortions came from the third and fourth ambiguities in design. Incomplete and inconsistent tinkering with market prices distorted, if not undermined, the operation of the so-called price mechanism. This outcome adversely affected versions of economic logic that require untrammelled price data for decision making. The demand schedules of pressure, which often contradicted those modes of reasoning, created even more conceptual static. All these distortions do not lend themselves to empirical verification, but the mental harassment they imposed was no less real. Taken with physical factor distortions, the campaign's first phase thus inflicted multiple injuries on the people and resources of Tanganyika.

Pushing "native" export production remained the administration's primary campaign concern until the late 1930s. Then several officers revamped the program to eliminate what they regarded as the major problems during phase one. Ultimate revenue objectives of the campaign stayed constant. But phase two, which officially began in 1938, embodied important changes in design and implementation. There was, however, continuity in impact. Phase two reinforced the adverse effects of phase one. The only change was a more detailed administrative response to some criticisms.

PHASE TWO: COORDINATING MAXIMUM PRODUCTION FROM "NATIVES" AND "NON-NATIVES"

Officers found at least four bothersome problems: imperfect direction from the center; aggravated relations with the "non-native" sector; unrefined goals; and uneven pressure on the spot. So the design of phase two incorporated projected solutions to all four inadequacies.

When Gillman referred to the campaign as "our Director of Agriculture's pet" and Lee wrote about the "activities of the Agriculture Department in stimulating native production," they touched on the most glaring weakness of phase one. Many officials and unofficials identified the campaign too much with one technical agency of the bureaucracy. This perception was not wholly accurate because most administrative officers on the spot participated in some way. But the campaign did not have a coordination coming from the purposeful cooperation of the center's technical and administrative branches. The Secretariat was, in short, only a casual partner with the Agriculture Department in campaign management. Those two agencies had to forge stronger links to remove criticism that the government was speaking inconsistently.

The proposed remedy for imperfect central direction was not a revision in structure. The aim was greater reliance on personal communication between two strategically placed bureaucrats, Director of Agriculture A. J. Wakefield and the Secretariat's Acting Administrative Secretary W. E. H. Scupham. These men had a particular stake in more effective implementation. Both belonged to that small group of officers that was redesigning the campaign. Before the administration inaugurated phase two, the group first had to deal with those other problems.

Better relations with various groups in the falsely stereotyped "non-native" sector required more than Harold MacMichael's gentlemen's agreement with Tanganyika sisal growers. Private ad hoc deals with special interests were not enough. Public assurances that a rejuvenated campaign would not harm supplies of African labor fell short. The administration had to take, or seem to take, a fairer stance toward the activities of all Tanganyika producers and translate greater equity into the campaign's design and implementation. The design part was easier. Phase two called on all producers, excluding again African coffee planters, to generate more output and promised fair and efficient coordination of all activity.

On paper this coordination extended a notion of economic complementarity proposed by Gov. Horace Byatt in 1921. He wrote, "I believe that production in this country will be most successful if it depends upon native industry for the smaller crops, such as cotton, cereals, and oil bearing seeds, and upon European capital for cotton-ginning and the growing of such commodities as sisal-fibre and flax, which need machinery and adequate capital for their preparation."[15] Wakefield and Scupham elaborated on this division of production in 1938. This also allowed them to address the problem of unrefined goals. Each province should concentrate on that combination of tasks that best exemplified their version of complementarity.

To define both complementarity and regional goals, the Secretariat issued a series of provincial profiles. Their thrust can be detected from several examples. Officers in the Southern Highlands Province, for instance, should work on four tasks: increasing food supplies for sale at the Lupa mining fields and to "natives" employed on the tea plantations; stimulating the labor supply to the gold-mining, tea, and pyrethrum industries; encouraging "native" cotton planting along the Iringa-Kilosa road; and extending rice cultivation in the lowland area of Iringa.[16]

Multiple duties applied elsewhere. Officers in the Central Province should facilitate movement of their migrant labor to the Northern and Tanga Provinces and encourage production of more foodstuffs. These were defined in a 1939 addendum as "mtama (sorghum) and uwele (bullrush millet) as well as sweet potatoes and cassava."[17] In the Lake Province, phase two should be a "straight native-crop matter," except in parts of Musoma, where the mines needed workers. Wakefield added, "I should not like to have natives who have been regularly employed in the mines in the vicinity of their homes induced to give up this work for cotton planting."[18] Wakefield suggested that officers in the Western Province promote expanded rice production for export and that their Northern counterparts encourage the coffee-growing Chagga to plant cotton, an appeal tried before with little success. The territorial sum of all provincial profiles would, those officers hoped, balance the demands of plantation and peasant agriculture, convincing critics of phase one that there was some equity in the phase two design.

The fourth administrative problem—uneven local pressure—was least amenable to revision. In 1938 the Secretariat issued clearer guidelines concerning how much pressure local officers might exert on Tanganyikans.[19] But the major proposal was to expand employment of European district crop supervisors throughout the territory. Three had begun work on a temporary basis in the Southern Province in 1934.

"It is a fact," Wakefield argued, "that the native works best under European supervision, the output of produce which can then be credited to him is considerably higher than that of the average peasant cultivator. So that if all the able-bodied Africans could be working on an organised plan under supervision there could be no talk to-day of lack of tonnage on the railways."[20] While Wakefield would have preferred to make these temporary district foremen permanent and to station them in as many prime "native" crop locations as possible, the Secretariat decided to retain their interim status but expand their employment in selected areas.

More effective communication between administrative and technical branches at all levels did make the implementation of phase two more efficient in some ways. Several actions were taken to improve relations with the "non-native" sector on the troublesome question of African labor supplies. Wakefield tried to tighten MacMichael's gentlemen's agreement with sisal producers. He asked cotton ginners not to distribute any seed in that area of no propaganda. "If any natives in that special plantation area want seed they must of course have it, but do not make it easy for them to get it, let them walk to the ginnery for it," he said.[21]

Facilitating timely flows of labor to the sisal estates in Morogoro and Kilosa districts also received attention. Wakefield instructed the district officer, the agricultural officer, and the labor inspectorate to examine the matter "after ascertaining the labour requirements of sisal estates in the vicinity," although "in no way should Government be recruiting agents or held responsible for supply of labour."[22] Government paid more attention in practice to the labor needs of some European coffee growers. Wakefield recounted for Scupham one episode of striking cooperation. He had just returned in late 1938 from an inspection tour that included Dodoma in the Central Province.

The usual complaint of "complete cessation of labour" has come from Anderson [a European coffee planter]. Partridge [the Chief Secretary] and I discussed this and he suggested that Anderson and Mauran [the President of the European Kilimanjaro Planters Association] go to Dodoma to discuss matters where I am sure some arrangement of benefit to the Administration, the coffee growers and the natives will be arranged, e.g. the Association to make known how many men they want and when they want them, this should enable District Officers so to time their tax drives to coincide with the months when labour is most required, also it is hoped to persuade at least the bigger employers to provide lorry transport.[23]

However, provincial profiles caused further problems for some local administrators. Revealing confidential evidence from the Western Province suggests difficulties there with multiple duties that surely occurred elsewhere. Mandated to increase rice and other crop production for export, plus maintain adequate food supplies, local officers found these demands imposed an unbearable burden upon farmers. In 1940, Provincial Commissioner O. G. Williams admitted that the last two seasonal drives were "not very successful" in increasing "economic crop or grain production." He blamed the weather to some extent. Then he reported how African cultivators in the Kahama and Tabora districts analyzed underproduction. To plant rice they first had to construct dams, which required time. The Native Authorities, fearing a food shortage, ordered every household to plant up to an acre of cassava. Dam construction, cassava planting, and rice cultivation made it difficult to increase production of other economic crops.[24] Unfavorable precipitation patterns did constrain yields; but those cultivators correctly analyzed another factor that undermined farming in every respect—the dispersion of too little labor over too many tasks too quickly.

While provincial profiles may have clarified the meaning of complementarity for both administrators and the administered, crop foremen defined the latter's role more forcibly. These supervisors did not receive a uniformly favorable reception from the regular staff. Provincial Commissioner A. E. Kitching, Southern, objected to their appointment because few "sound" people would work for twenty-five pounds a month; these would be the dregs, "usually unemployable by private enterprise in normal times." Wakefield countered, "There were good types of Greeks, Seychellians, and Mauritanis with a lower standard of living than British and 25 pounds was regarded as satisfactory."[25]

D. A. G. Dallas, district officer for Rufiji, offered this mixed assessment of their performance, ". . . despite their many admirable qualities, Europeans having any tincture of levantine blood carry no weight in the Rufiji or any other coastal district." He asked for "genuine western European cotton supervision."[26] Such a racial "upgrading" was impossible, because the Secretariat decided to terminate the experiment with special crop supervisors for "financial reasons." This rationale summarized publicly several privately circulating discontents. Some believed that the administration was not getting its money's worth in increased production from this specialized application of pressure. Others probably felt that specialization itself, as well as the identities of those supervisors, departed from the more civilized manipulation associated with indirect administration.

Some local officers regretted the end of the experiment. Captain Frank Hallier, Provincial Commissioner, Northern, wrote to the Administrative Secretary: "Scup, they are needed to stimulate indolent Mbugwe, whose practice it is to pick just enough [cotton] to pay their tax and no more, to pick more [cotton]." Their withdrawal has "dimmed prospect of a record crop."[27]

In its wider impact phase two reinforced the distortions wrought by phase one—the misallocation of physical factors, for example. Criticism that the campaign still encouraged land abuse prompted official rebuttal from Director Wakefield in 1939. "Over a great part of the Territory," he asserted, "there should be little if any danger of unbridled exploitation of the soil from any campaign for the increased production of crops." Take the Morogoro district, he argued. If every family planted half an acre of cotton, representing about fifteen man-days' work, only 24,000 acres would be required for production. Whether land suitable for cotton planting was available in that quantity did not trouble the Director. Nor did he concede that soil exhaustion was harmful, even when he admitted its imminence in the Lake Province. In fact, he felt this threat was beneficial, because it would accelerate the adoption of more intensive methods of farming and manuring.[28]

Whether or not the campaign's short-run harms were long-term blessings by the administration's own reckoning, the people then living still had to contend with its immediate consequences. Distorted labor allocation continued as another persistent reminder of the campaign's operation. Actual experience with phase two in the Western Province showed what fragmentation in activity the campaign could induce. A more efficient implementation probably did little to diminish distortions in communication. Provincial profiles were still too general to reduce problems associated with inexact microeconomic production targets. Crop supervisors generally applied persuasion with greater consistency, but this result intensified existing conflicts between prices and pressures.

By its distortions the "plant-more-crops" campaign added more forms of underdevelopment in Tanganyika. Two deserve re-emphasis. First, entangling oral, juridical, and physical pressures with market price signals confused economic communication, and doing it inconsistently caused major damage. Second, consider again the impact of administrative intervention in local food markets.

For most bureaucrats local food supplies had two meanings: what was available within a particular district and what an individual household might produce to feed itself. Colonial legislation and boundaries sustained these perceptions. In times of actual or expected food shortage, Native Authorities, citing their own 1923 enabling ordinance, mandated actions that verged on extreme economic autarky: the household should become as food self-sufficient as possible.[29]

Faced with the same conditions, administrative officers, in addition to speaking through the Native Authorities, could also invoke directly a 1924 ordinance that empowered them to embargo food exports from a district and to regulate supplies within it. Implementing this split-level interpretation of local as only household and district retarded the emergence of food markets that transcended those categories. Developing exchange patterns in food would have suffered less damage if administrative decisions had not so often prevented the extension of local markets, whether they consisted of several households or entire villages in the same district or across boundaries. These are, of course, musings after the fact. Households, administrators reasoned, could most easily estimate their own food requirements; besides, they were easy to spot-check for compliance with compulsory planting edicts.

In their own criticisms of the "plant-more-crops" campaign, several Colonial Office officials considered internal food production and local distribution as related questions. G. L. M. Clauson argued, "By organizing an interchange of goods and services *within* the territory everyone ought to be put into a position of having enough to eat and decent houses to live in . . . emphasis ought to be laid on the growing of foodstuffs, the evolution of native staffs and so on and the production for export should take second place." "I agree with Mr. Clauson," H. Tempany wrote in 1939: ". . . the greater the extent to which the dependence of the Territory on imported food can be reduced the greater will be the margin of exchange available for the purchase abroad of services and articles which cannot be supplied locally. . . ."[30]

These were not the strategies of the "plant-more-crops" campaign, nor of the territorial bureaucracy in general, whose economic approaches worked against the horizontal integration of various levels of local exchange advocated by Clauson and Tempany.

The next two chapters probe the enveloping web of commodity regulation, and show how regulation affected individuals personally and as members of groups.

7

Regulating the Cotton Industry:
The Futility of Paper Protest

I N organizing the cotton industry, the Tanganyika administration followed strategies and prescribed rules that affected various groups in different ways. Because regulation and local response become more complicated in the 1930s, this chapter concentrates on that decade. To make a technical subject interesting, this chapter features a case study and a series of local vignettes. The arena of protest with the richest written evidence was the Eastern Province, from 1935 through 1939. There some cotton producers criticized government market organization and price manipulation with little visible result for themselves but with significant benefits for this study. Testimony shows witnesses explaining what they thought government intervention was doing and, with other vignettes, sketches the impact of regulation on commodities and people. The strategy and limited regulation of the 1920s set the stage for a portrayal of forces behind more concerted intervention, which prompted zoning and other devices to control competition in the early 1930s.

SETTING THE STAGE: THE WANING OF COMPETITION
IN COTTON BUYING

Although the first rules prescribing grades for the marketing of African cotton appeared in the 1920s, the administration was more concerned with stimulating production of a sometimes "unpopular"[1] crop than with its purchase, transport, and distribution. But local officers resisted outside attempts to manipulate and channel their own exhortations. The most important conflict occurred in the early 1920s between A. H. Kirby, then Director of Agriculture, and representatives of the Empire Cotton Growing Corporation (ECGC). The basic issue was whether the bureaucracy should spread or concentrate its efforts to encourage cotton production. Kirby favored an extensive approach; the ECGC wanted concentration on five districts. "Experience has shown," he argued, "that [an] increase of cotton production among natives can be most quickly brought about by extensive work in as many developable areas as possible. Intensive work concentrated in a few districts is slow to give [a] large increase of production, on account of lack of population and the nature of the producer to be dealt with. . . ."[2] Kirby's reasoning prevailed; the ECGC withdrew from Tanganyika. This dispute merely capped its disenchantment with government policy.[3]

While regulation of cotton markets and prices did not accelerate until the 1930s, an isolated harbinger of greater intervention appeared in 1924 when the bureaucracy granted a monopoly license for the purchase of cotton in the Moshi district. Both the Indian Association and African producers strongly protested this creation of a monopsony. But Acting Governor John Scott was "satisfied that monopoly though in principle undesirable was necessary this year in order to foster infant industry by assuring [a] definite market at [a] fixed price."[4] Even though this action only affected one district for one year, the reaction it provoked foreshadowed a rocky reception for similar future moves.

Competition among buyers of African cotton was, by most accounts, keen in the early and mid-1920s but began to decline in the late 1920s. In many locations buyers entered into collusive agreements to reduce or eliminate competition among themselves. This diminution was occurring at the same time the government was experiencing internal conflicts on how best to organize the cotton industry. The Cotton Advisory Board (CAB), created in 1927 as another satellite agency with mixed official-unofficial membership, was in tandem with the Secretariat at the beginning of 1930 on the need to control competition in a stable way. Because of cheating and enforcement difficulties, private collusion was precarious and unlikely to accomplish this. On January 9, 1930, the Board was "unable to accept the view that the erection of ginneries and the establishment of cotton markets can be governed by the anticipation of profit by private investors"; it gave "unqualified support to the principle adopted by the Government that these activities must be controlled though this must result in the restriction of private enterprise, and individuals or Companies may thereby be prevented from investing capital in accordance with their wishes." The Board's policy was, in short, to "protect the ginnery from uneconomic competition by other buyers," which connoted "generally the exclusion of the middleman from areas in which he does not already exist." This policy was based on "assurances" from the Board's chairman, the Director of Agriculture, that his department could protect the producer "to the extent of ensuring he receives a fair price" and could "require every ginnery, ginnery buying post, or auction market to buy on an agreed scale of prices."[5]

But on April 11, 1930, the CAB proposed a more restrictive solution to the problem of uneconomic competition, which provoked dissent from Governor Cameron. The Board recommended, "In the future no cotton market plots be disposed of except to ginners."[6] Cameron rejected this proposal, insisting the Government must work to preserve an "element of competition" in cotton buying. He added, "If possible that competition should be between ginneries through buying posts, but where this is impossible there should be a small measure of dilution by means of cotton market plots."[7] And until he left the governorship in 1931, he restrained the CAB from implementing its more extreme proposals for reducing the number of cotton buyers. Cameron's departure removed the most powerful official advocate of an "element of competition."

Those preoccupied with eliminating uneconomic competition soon had their day. These people, both officials and unofficials in Tanganyika as well as England, agreed on the desirability of zoning. Zoning meant demarcating areas within the territory, based on administrative divisions, and restricting the number of cotton buyers to what the CAB deemed optimal for each location. In their common solution, different people emphasized distinct but overlapping rationales. At an Eastern Province Cotton Conference in Dar es Salaam, on December 8, 1932, Mr. C. A. Callander of Liverpool Uganda Co. (Ltd.), representing the Tanganyika Ginneries Association, advocated zoning as a solution to four interwoven problems. These were: too many ginneries in relation to output, the "high cost" of buying "native cotton" occasioned by "excessive competition," the "unreasonably high price" paid to planters for inferior cotton, and the unnecessary transport of seed cotton from district to district.[8]

Over one month later, on January 12, 1933, the CAB noted the gathering pressure for zoning from outside the territory. Its deliberations, Chairman Harrison reported to the Chief Secretary, were "tending in the direction of zoning as in accordance with the representations made to the S of S [Secretary of State for Colonies] by those interested in the cotton industry in Britain."

But Harrison put the rationale for zoning in a somewhat different way: its objective was "to devise a sufficiently strong local interest in the cotton crop to enable ginners and cotton buyers to support growers."[9] On February 19, 1934, he noted that zoning should "meet some of the disabilities under which cotton growers and ginners seemed to labor." One major disability was the independent cotton buyer "attaining a position of dominance" in the industry, which adversely affected many planters and ginners. For Harrison, the ". . . grower was the person who was deprived of the real price for his cotton by having to carry an organisation too expensive and too complex for the crop, and to secure what were called competitive prices, he had to pay handsomely for the fiction." A comprehensive solution to these disabilities required not only zoning but also price controls of the kind called feasible by the Director of Agriculture in 1930. For the grower "the price factor must be considered, but . . . it must not be too dominant." Harrison concluded, "We want a regular and increasing planting and production on merit, fair dealing, and fair returns, not on belated enthusiasm."[10]

From 1933 on there unfolded a complicated pattern of regulation. The administration zoned more and more districts and set prices every week. Prices were based on the full price of Liverpool middling four months cotton futures, with certain charges deducted.[11] The following stories examine some implications of price manipulation and market organization.

PAPER PROTEST IN THE EASTERN PROVINCE

In early 1935 the Secretariat received two letters that, although allegedly coming from different groups, were identical at some points in language.[12] On February 28 some African cotton planters wrote to the Chief Secretary from Kilosa. They said, "We understand that the Existing Cotton Markets will be abolished in the near future in this District. . . ." Their premise was that "the Establishment of Cotton Markets Means Competetion, and from competetion there will be better prices offered to us for our Seed-Cotton; and this will be most encouraging and of great usefull to us." These growers complained about the forces oppressing them. The first was the bureaucracy: "We are continuously asked to plant more and more cotton, and also we are pressed for our Hut and Poll Tax. . . ." The second was the oligopsony represented by the ginners: ". . . they are only buyers in those areas where no markets exist." They pressed their own demands: "In establishing Cotton Markets, where there will be competetive prices, we are certain to obtain better prices than that offered by the ginners and their buying posts. . . ."[13] Five people signed this letter, among whom were Saleh Yusuf Mkoma, Saleke Amari, and Abdullah bin Selemani. The Acting Chief Secretary wrote Mkoma on March 8 that the "matter is receiving consideration."[14]

On February 23 the African Planters Association (APA) wrote the Chief Secretary from Morogoro. Although this document precedes the Kilosa letter by five days, the Kilosa background will prove helpful. The APA took aim at Government Notice No. 73 of July 17, 1934, which closed areas in the Morogoro district to the transport and sale of seed cotton. This action was "very detrimental," the letter said, adding, ". . . we are obliged to deliver our seed-cotton at the ginneries and at the ginnery buying posts existing in the closed areas at the prices offered to us by the buyers at these posts, although Government has fixed a minimum scale which it is considered is a fair price, we feel sure that we would obtain better prices if cotton markets [were] established in the areas where there are none." It continued, "If we were free to carry our seed-cotton in the Morogoro district and to sell it to whomsoever we like, we will be in a better position, we think, to judge where we should deliver it and obtain better prices; and not be obliged to deliver it to the only buyers available in the areas, viz: the ginners and their buying posts."[15] This letter was signed by the Secretary of the African Planters Association, Kibwana Riwamba, and its President, Salim Seif Longone. The Acting Chief Secretary wrote the APA on March 12 that the "matter is receiving consideration."[16]

There were striking similarities between the letters. Morogoro's fourth paragraph was identical to Kilosa's third, excepting the substitution "of great advantage to us" for "of great usefull to us." The first part of Morogoro's fifth paragraph replicates Kilosa's fourth, but Morogoro expands on the plea to be released from transport restrictions. And so on. Harrison had one explanation for the overlap: ". . . the signatories are not store owners, but no doubt have been moved to write, by the middlemen." Whatever the origins of those letters, initial inside consideration of their arguments is revealing. Harrison again argued that producers were better off in an environment of controlled prices and purchasing than before. However, a final clause implies that minimum prices may not always be fair: "The prices natives are now getting under the scale are quite 3 if not 5 cents per kilogram more than they would have obtained, had we not applied the minimum price, now formed up to a fair price."[17]

Although administered prices diverged from some conceptions of fairness, officers from the affected area insisted producers benefited from regulation. On March 14 Provincial Commissioner G. F. Webster, Eastern, reported, "Both the D. O., Kilosa, with whom I have discussed the matter, and I are in favour of the abolition of cotton markets which encourage large numbers of middlemen into the cotton industry. Well distributed buying posts, at which minimum prices have to be paid for the purchase of cotton by licensed ginners or their agents, would I think be true." Neither Harrison nor Webster could forget an agreement that Eastern Province ginners and middlemen made in 1932 on commission and transport allowances, which allegedly reduced cotton prices five cents per kilogram "everywhere," and the three cents per kilogram increase that price regulation secured almost "at once."[18] For Webster, administered prices remained a bulwark protecting producers. He noted, "During the last season in the Kilosa District, only the fixed minimum prices were paid at all markets."[19]

The signatories apparently had one community of interest with some Indian traders. The *Tanganyika Opinion (Daily)* and *Tanganyika Herald*, which reflected their attitudes to some extent, commented on the protest. On March 23 the *Opinion* said the question was "freedom to sell" and saw portents in the trend of government market organization. The newspaper commented: "Strong suspicion still persists in the mind of the Indian community against the system of grant of monopolies for purchase of native produce. Monopolies are believed to be a weapon which could be turned against the Indian without appearing to do so."[20] On the same day, the *Herald* printed the Morogoro letter and called it a "smashing answer to the Government plea that monopoly is necessary in the interest of native growers." The editors of the *Herald* believed the Government could not afford to overlook the fact that African planters "are sophisticated enough to show a deep concern for their own affairs." They praised "free trade" as a cause of Uganda's growth; Africans there supposedly planted more cotton because a minimum price scale was not enforced.[21] On March 29 the *Herald* thought that the revised CAB unofficial roster would deprive middlemen of their representation and asserted, "With the views of middlemen the Native cotton growers are in full agreement."[22]

Meanwhile, the APA was becoming restless. On March 26 its leaders wrote the Chief Secretary, "We beg to invite your attention to your letter No. 10844/453 dated 12th inst. and respectfully beg to request you to please now give us reply."[23] The bureaucracy was in no hurry. Sometime in March Harrison shared his own thoughts on the original Morogoro letter with the Chief Secretary—the technical issues it raised as well as the problems the APA presented. His stand on relations between markets and prices was more dogmatic. Harrison said: "The establishment of cotton markets has not resulted in higher prices to the grower than are promulgated by the fair price scale. The assertion that were there more markets, there would be more competition is not historically true, what we have found is that higher prices are put on the board but the native does not necessarily get these higher prices, however good they may appear to be." His assessment of the APA indicated that difficult times were ahead for the Association: "The grievances stated are more imaginary than real, and the tenor of the letter indicates to me that its production has been induced. Furthermore, the association under reference is hardly in a position to form any valuable opinion and I would respectfully recommend that its pretensions be examined."[24]

Examining its pretensions soon included a strategy of harassment. The Solicitor General outlined his thinking, "The rules of this particular association [APA] . . . provide the organizers with opportunities for exploitation and malpractice of a kind with which I was very familiar in the Gold Coast, and they usually get away with the proceeds . . ." However, "there was nothing illegal in such organizations," and "if there were any hope of their transactions being conducted in a business-like and honest manner, they should prove beneficial." And then the key strategy: "I doubt whether it would be feasible to avoid the formation of such associations by legislation, and in the absence of a prohibiting enactment the best way to discourage them is to prosecute the organisers when in the fullness of time their activities become criminal."[25]

All the while, those planters were patiently orchestrating their grievances within administrative structures. The Kilosa group had sent another letter on April 8, which elicited a May 18 reply from the Acting Chief Secretary. The response said arrangements for cotton marketing "will be those which experience has proved to be most advantageous to the industry as a whole," and "they will, as at present, safeguard the interests of the producer."[26] On the same day the Secretariat forwarded an identical letter (excepting, of course, the reference was to "yours of 23rd February") to the President of the African Planters Association, Morogoro.

By mid-May 1935, the administration had prepared its version of what happened to the APA dues but followed a strategy which did not include actual prosecution. D. C. Campbell, Acting Chief Secretary, reported, "The greater part of the money collected has been given out as unsecured loans to the so-called Committee members of the Association"; the Provincial Commissioner had taken the balance of 243 shillings on deposit. Campbell alleged that the "assistant treasurer at Kimamba had collected Shs. 395/50, giving receipts for Shs. 352; he remitted Shs. 200 to the Morogoro Association, used Shs. 139/50 himself, and had a balance of Shs. 56." The District Officer had taken this balance "on deposit," along with Shs. 85 recovered by selling the assistant treasurer's house. The Provincial Commissioner recommended, Campbell noted, that dues should be refunded, as far as possible, to the subscribers.[27] The Secretariat endorsed this action; it "should be done so far as possible in the presence of the subscribers to whom it might be explained how their money is being wasted."[28]

While the bureaucracy waited for this harassment to debilitate the

APA, it faced other irritants coming from that protest. Gov. Harold Mac-Michael had asked for a short note on the Morogoro matter that he could use at the League of Nations Mandates Commission meeting in Geneva, Switzerland. There, according to Deputy Chief Secretary Sayers, "Undue attention is paid to protests emanating from a handful of ignorant and misguided people!"[29] The prepared paper reprised the official line. Restricting the movement of unginned cotton from certain areas "prevents the spread of disease, enables the Agriculture Department to obtain unmixed seed for distribution to growers, reduces overhead charges, and eliminates unnecessary transport." The presence of cotton markets "with middlemen buyers has not resulted in the payment of higher prices to the grower than the minimum fixed by Government." And the Association "represents only a small number of the native cotton growers of the District."[30]

This "handful of ignorant and misguided people" did not succumb to initial administrative pressure. On August 24, 1935, the Kilosa growers petitioned the Governor, restating their complaints about market reorganization in more detail but now emphasizing a contradiction in price regulation that the bureaucracy had trouble explaining. Price manipulation should promote fair and stable rewards for growers, but linking local cotton prices to a discounted version of Liverpool futures struck some officers as unfair and this device did little for stability. Prices still fluctuated, and planters criticized the contradiction. Commenting on the Kilosa petition, an unidentified Secretariat member observed, "Every attempt has been made to explain the reasons for the fluctuations on the Liverpool market."

The administration researched the backgrounds of the twelve who signed the August 24 Kilosa petition and the unidentified Secretariat member summarized the results: "The natives whose names are signed to this petition are those who cultivate areas of cotton sufficiently large to necessitate the employment of labour." This fact suggested an analysis of producer discontent: "Natives who grow half an acre or more [sic] can manage their crop without labour and therefore reap the full benefit from the sale thereof, whilst they do not suffer loss of capital should their crop prove unsuccessful." As consolation to an administration whose visions of stability included a homogeneous African peasantry, the member concluded, "The peasant producer appears satisfied with his cotton activities but the employer of labour is dissatisfied."[31]

In early September Governor MacMichael considered the Kilosa document of August 24. "This petition has no doubt been answered dozens of times before," he thought, "and somebody can tell me what the answer should be."[32] The answer was, of course, no. On September

11 Acting Chief Secretary Campbell wrote the Provincial Commissioner, Eastern, asking him to inform the petitioners that "H. E. is unable to accede to their requests."[33] To give the Commissioner a rationale for rejection, Campbell quoted from the note the Secretariat prepared for the Governor's use at Geneva.

Several months after this experience with communication up and down a hierarchy, the growers tried again. On January 13, 1936, the African Planters Association, Morogoro and Kilosa, wrote the Chief Secretary. Whether this new masthead represented a formal merger of two distinct groups or the abandonment of multiple protests by one united organization is not known. If the title was new, the grievances were familiar. The Association referred to the Secretariat's letter of May 18, 1935, and repeated that closing areas of the Morogoro district was detrimental. The letter said, "What we desire is that any native may take his seed cotton to whatever market or store he chooses to sell it." The planters introduced more evidence to support their arguments. In the Kissaki area cotton was grown abundantly but had no market, only buying posts attached to the Duthumi ginnery. As the ginners are the only buyers, the price "naturally is the exact minimum fixed by Government." The writers asked the Government to help Africans and the cotton industry move beyond a situation in which only a few benefit, "the ginners and their buying agents."[34] Campbell responded on January 23 that "this subject is now under consideration by Government and . . . your Association's representations will be borne in mind."[35]

The APA waited several more months, then called at the central offices of the Agriculture Department, located in Morogoro. N. V. Rounce, an officer in the department, met with the deputation on April 16, recorded their requests and analysis, and forwarded a summary to his director. They asked again for permission to sell their cotton outside the district and its "syndicate of ginners." If the Government could not grant this request, they wanted clearance to erect a ginnery themselves. They said, "Although Government could not avoid the formation of rings or syndicates, at the same time the combination of these with zoning, came to the same thing as the Government pointing to a single merchant and saying 'you must sell to him alone.' " They did "not think this was what Government had in its mind when formulating the zoning policy." Hence, "they had made numerous representations to Government, but without result."[36]

Their perseverance brought results, but of a different kind. On April 24 District Officer E. E. Hutchins, Morogoro, wrote Acting Director Wakefield that the president of the Association believed there were now 210 members in the vicinity of Morogoro and Mikese [Mikesse]. "He was last year warned against extending the Association's sphere of influence,'' Hutchins observed, ''but states that there are now about a hundred Turiani natives and between 280–300 at Kisaki anxious to join.''[37] There is no way to verify actual and potential membership estimates, but the fact of increasing police surveillance was real.

Wakefield maintained official lines in a confidential letter to the Chief Secretary on April 23. The Association was small and a tool of the middlemen. As Wakefield noted, ''There is no doubt that the representatives of this Association, of less than 50 native cotton growers in the vicinity of Morogoro township, out of a total number of 11,000 growers for the Morogoro District for the year 1935, have been directly inspired by middlemen.'' The arguments that the APA presented in its January 13 letter were ''rather contradictory.'' For Wakefield the contradiction came from juxtaposing these examples; the APA had built its case on the first. In Kisaki middlemen were excluded and there cotton production increased; in Morogoro, where ''middlemen have full play,'' cotton production decreased.[38] Most intriguing in that letter was an ''example of the secret agreements and machinations of middlemen and ginners in this area to the disturbance of the native growers.'' One of the leading middlemen in Morogoro was financially interested in the Mikesse ginnery, which the East African Cotton Company (EACC) had purchased in 1934 after zoning was instituted. ''It is the aim of this Company to purchase cotton in Kisaki and Turiani areas, where the APA has no members, as far as I know.''[39] The Director presumably believed that the leading middleman was pushing the APA protest to change zoning patterns in the Kisaki and Turiani areas. That unidentified middleman desired to become a ginner, possibly in some kind of association with the EACC, which itself had argued repeatedly that zoning was ''unfair,'' and which might benefit if permitted to operate in those new areas.

Although this particular episode cannot be corroborated, many middlemen were striving to become ginners, and some were making it, at least in the east. The Eastern Province Cotton Buyers Association (EPCBA), a middlemen's group, lost a voice on the Cotton Advisory Board in the mid-1930s when the Government eliminated the seat for a middleman representative of the Eastern Province cotton industry.[40] The Secretary of the EPCBA insisted it would continue to exist, since it ''derives its strength . . . from rapacity of ginners who want to eliminate [the] small man . . .'' But with a self-revelation unusual in a lobbyist's letter to government, the Secretary admitted that the Association confronted one major danger: the ''evolution that was taking place from buyers to ginners.''[41]

While the bureaucracy downgraded the EPCBA, it responded to

some aspects of the APA protest in an indirect and limited way. At the March 24, 1937, meeting of the Cotton Advisory Board in Morogoro, Chairman Harrison explained that, although there was not sufficient cotton produced in the Morogoro and Kilosa districts to justify the retention of middlemen, "it would be politic to do." The Board decided to retain one "open market" in each district at which three ginners and three middlemen could buy, and it approved all middlemen licenses for the 1937/38 season in the Eastern Province. But an updating of ginnery zones, which Harrison declared on June 10, 1937, did not remove the taproot of subdistrict grievance. Three ginneries (Msowero, Rudewa, and Kilosa) were to serve Kilosa district. Harrison zoned Turiani and Duthumi areas in Morogoro district for only one ginnery each but assigned the rest of the district to the Ngerengere, Mikesse, and Morogoro ginneries.[42]

These actions did not satisfy the protesters. On April 5, 1938, they again wrote the Chief Secretary in their endeavors to break the "ginners' syndicate" or get permission to construct their own ginnery.[43] The administration soon decided to favor existing ginners even more as part of the second phase of the "plant-more-crops" campaign. The notion of complementarity, key to the coordination that phase two promised, did not include most middlemen in the cotton industry. The administration never publicly announced what Director Wakefield wrote in confidence to the Chief Secretary on October 21, 1938. In phase two, "It will be vitally important to ensure the co-operation of ginneries," he noted. "Because the middlemen will play no part in the campaign, the ginners will do so more enthusiastically if they know they will get the bulk of the cotton."[44] At a meeting of ginners in Morogoro, November 12, 1938, Wakefield argued that there "were no half-measures: either cut-throat competition or no competition" in cotton buying; ". . . in fact progress [for the cotton industry] has been most sound in those ginnery zones where competition had never existed."[45]

From an administration bent on further reducing competition in cotton buying, the APA experienced greater frustrations. On March 20, 1939, six members wrote the Chief Secretary revealing their plight: "We your subjects remind you that our letter of the 5th April, 1938, in which we were sorry to have to ask your help has not yet been answered. Did not it reach you? (We enclose another copy.)" The writers continued: "We have heard that there will be a cotton meeting on the 39th [sic] of March and we six people accordingly sent our names to you so that we can come to this meeting, but we have not yet had an answer nor has our District Officer, Kilosa, given us a reply, and we notice that the 39th is very near. Accordingly we remind you in case you can help us and give us rail tickets so that we can be in time for the meeting. The tickets should be addressed to the District Officer, Kilosa, to enable us to set off quickly.''[46] The Secretariat's reply was brief. Writing to Saleh bin Yusuf on April 1, 1939, the Acting Chief Secretary responded that, with reference to the March 20 letter stating no reply had been received to the letter of April 5, 1938, ''a copy of a reply which was sent to that letter is now enclosed.''[47]

That is the final recorded exchange between the APA and the Tanganyika administration to be found. Suffocated by red tape and oppressed by police surveillance, the Association may have collapsed altogether or so dwindled that its activities warranted no further scrutiny from the Secretariat. Whatever the APA's fate, its protest touched on most essential features of cotton regulation and exposed several key problems about the intervention. In the final section of this chapter those issues are discussed against an Eastern Province background enriched by other local vignettes.

IMPLICATIONS OF REGULATION FOR COMMODITIES AND PEOPLE

Setting minimum prices and limiting the number of buyers through zoning left the administration open to valid criticisms. The Government was, of course, a threshold price setter for monopsonies. For oligopsonies the Government became, in effect, the price leader for ginners or combinations of ginners and middlemen wishing to collude. By eliminating one major problem for private coalitions—what price to set—and by making the size of groups feasible for cooperation—through reduced numbers—the Government almost encouraged such formations. Eastern Province experience confirmed this result. ''Even when middlemen are associated in buying,'' Secretariat member A. Sillery commented in 1936, ''a ring agreement exists and the minimum promulgated price is paid so that no advantage results to the producer from the presence of middlemen.''[48] The same trend appeared elsewhere. ''It has been observed,'' wrote the Secretary of the Middlemen and Cotton Growers Society, Ltd., to the Director of Agriculture in 1937, ''both in Uganda and here that on the State prescribing a formula for a minimum price the ginning interests have taken to forming a ring for the purchase of cotton and to pay the minimum price only.''[49]

The Secretary referred only to ginning interests and did not mention middlemen. In Tanganyika many ginner oligopsonists preferred to collude without them so they set out to eliminate any middlemen in their vicinity.[50] The Government's occasional decision to allow equal numbers of middlemen's and ginners' stores in the same location could help. The premise was that equal numbers preserved a semblance of competition, but an episode in the Lake Province showed how vulnerable individual middlemen were to the machinations of collaborating ginners. In Sukumaland the Government elevated two markets, which had been only Produce (Ginners) Markets, to the status of Produce (Cotton) Markets and sold middlemen as many store plots as occupied by ginners. This action was a mistake, reported Senior Agricultural Officer D. Sturdy in January 1938, "since in actual fact during this season middlemen competition was completely eradicated, and the Ginners appeared to obtain full control of all buying stores." There the ginners were too entrenched for any minor mandated element of competition to upset them.

Many growers might not have found reductions in selling options so disturbing had the administration manipulated prices differently. Even within its own frames of reference, minimum prices were unstable, sometimes unfair, and often uneconomic as well. Officer Sturdy, whose thinking did not mimic the Harrison-Wakefield line, supported economic price as one of three policy changes he recommended after the Sukumaland incident. The Government should concentrate more on the producer, promote "bigger markets," and make the buyers "pay not a minimum but an economic price as in Uganda," he said.[51] Economic prices, though perhaps not as high as the excessive ones buyers alleged they had to pay in the 1920s, might still have functioned as more effective producer incentives than Tanganyika's minimum prices, even when "formed up" to fairness.[52]

But those who set policy seemed impervious to most suggestions.[53] Later in 1938 Wakefield zoned the Southern Province for familiar reasons. Zoning was necessary to control Mikindani ginnery owners, he reported. These people were trying to penetrate an area served by the Mtua ginnery and were "tempting the natives" by offering higher prices. "As can be imagined," Wakefield wrote the Southern Provincial Commissioner, "this upset the native grower and such tactics can only do harm to the industry." By zoning the ginneries, "the owners will look more to the development of the areas assigned to them rather than to irresponsible meddling in areas outside their economic sphere."[54]

Even when creating stable conditions for collusion, the Government argued that minimum prices protected growers from harmful buyer machinations. The administered price was in some cases higher than what private agreements had produced before greater regulation (the 1932 Eastern Province pact). But many rings were inherently unstable. Had the Government not intervened, some rings would have disintegrated, price competition would have revived in those locations, and growers there might have more than made up for returns depressed by collusion. For local producers and distributors, these were idle speculations. No wonder an "evolution that was taking place from buyers to ginners." No wonder a prescient proposal in 1932 suggested that Native Administrations in some Lake Province districts take over ginneries from the British Cotton Growing Association and run these on a cooperative basis. The Government rejected this suggestion, as it would frustrate the APA request to operate a ginnery.[55]

And what, in the end, did the APA protest mean? Here was an organization of African growers, whose inner circle probably never exceeded twenty people and whose total membership by most favorable reckoning remained in the low hundreds, working for change within the Tanganyika administrative system. Helped at times by some Indian middlemen who found overlapping grievances, the APA was the creation of African planters running farms that required hired labor. No longer small-scale peasant farmers but emerging cotton capitalists, these people found regulation onerous because they could have afforded to search for the best deal in a less restricted environment. Their arguments became more sophisticated. At the outset they believed that increasing the number of buyers and markets would lead to more price competition in their vicinity. But they were right that restrictions on movement prevented them from taking advantage of price differentials that might have existed elsewhere. As the protest unfolded, they criticized minimum prices more, because it was this vise of prices and zoning that really squeezed them. And their final plea for permission to open a ginnery, which would have involved a partial vertical integration of the cotton industry, was a rational solution to their entrapment.[56]

But they trusted the force of arguments on paper, made to a bureaucracy that wore them out. Such was neither the strategy nor the result of the unrest that intensified around Mount Kilimanjaro in the Northern Province during the 1930s. There and then unfolded the complicated case study of inter-war protest that is explained in chapter 8.

8

Regulating the Coffee Industry:
A Warning from the Mountain

U N L I K E cotton, "native" coffee production, especially of the *arabica* variety, did not need much administrative encouragement. Acting Director of Agriculture Wolfe wrote in 1927 about "the Usambara natives being infected with the vogue for coffee growing now spreading among natives on Kilimanjaro. . . ."[1] And Acting Provincial Commissioner G. F. Webster, Northern, observed in 1928 that a person with a half acre of coffee, "which occupies very little of his time, can reap 5 cwts. per annum of high quality coffee (yield per acre ½ ton) which he can sell locally at Shs. 72/– per cwt. or Shs. 360/–.'' Though growers dispute his estimate of "very little" labor time, few in Tanganyika could deny Webster's conclusions. He said, "The natives are fully alive to the benefits of coffee growing,'' and added, "No other economic crop will give [them] anything approaching such a profit."[2]

So powerful an economic change coming from people themselves presented the Tanganyika administration with major control problems. While most problems appeared where "native" coffee growing was spreading,[3] these all converged with special force in the Northern Province, particularly in the Moshi district during the 1930s. The issues are presented here in the following story. The cleverness of some Chagga and the tactical errors of some British furnished material which makes this story fascinating. Several key facts about the Northern Province, the bureaucracy's chief trouble spot before World War II, are needed to set the stage.

THE NORTH: AN ARENA OF COMPETITION

The north was an arena of competition in at least three ways: among local societies, between the races, and among the Chagga people. One main theater was coffee production. Here competition was sharp because Africans and Europeans were growing the same type of coffee, the mountain-grown, richer-tasting *arabica,* which usually brought higher returns than *robusta*. In this dimension of competition, economic activity diverged greatly from the premise of complementarity, which emphasized cooperation. Had Africans in the north concentrated on *robusta* and Europeans on *arabica*, complementarity would have been preserved. However, its retention would not necessarily have spared the bureaucracy the trouble that was to come. The disharmony involved extensive litigation and at least twice flared into rioting. Origins lie as much in the errors of the administration, here indicted in its own terms, as in the shifting relationships of individuals, families, and subchiefdoms among the Chagga.

The Chagga coffee-growing industry represented an increasing and potentially destabilizing aggregation of power in the 1920s. Because the growth of that industry has been traced elsewhere,[4] this chapter stresses the traits that made many Chagga such formidable competitors. Many demonstrated a discriminating selectivity in their choice of techniques.[5] Many refused to imitate their European *arabica*-growing counterparts and thus saved themselves from agrarian mediocrity.[6] And many rejected a predominant administrative view of good agriculture as maximizing the production of individual crops. Instead they perceived their environment as an integral whole in which all crops and all labor activities contributed to strengthening whatever microeconomic community each deemed most dear.

The Chagga coffee-growing industry required a controlling administrative grid; a serious search for the appropriate structure took place, marked by some experimentation. Once a general decision was made, the administration debated the timing and manner of its implementation. This search was influenced by the actions of some Chagga, some British officers, and other Europeans, and especially by the consequences of their activity.

FINE-TUNING COOPERATIVE ORGANIZATION

A major problem concerned selecting the most desirable level of cooperative organization. In the early and mid-1920s Officer Charles C. F. Dundas assisted in the development of cultivators' associations in each Chagga chiefdom.[7] The mode of organization was, in its roots, locational and sub-tribal, but these associations joined to form the Kilimanjaro Native Planters Association (KNPA) in 1925.[8] What happened to and in the KNPA forced the administration to think through the problem of stability in relation to level of organization. Despite a public call in the late 1920s and early 1930s for cooperative organization based on the "tribal system,"[9] this hallowed axiom of indirect administration did not prevent the bureaucracy from manipulating the levels of localism inherent in most African societies to gain stability.

In one way the administration created its own problem. Unable to supervise the marketing of Chagga coffee in every respect, local officers brought in an outside firm, Messrs. C. C. Monckton and Company, to handle that job. By misjudging foreign coffee prices, that firm created a financial shortfall for the KNPA, which threatened its survival. The deterioration alone would have prompted reassessment of the bureaucracy's relations with the KNPA.[10] What made reconsideration of its structure urgent were events within and surrounding the Association.

The KNPA assisted in the rise of Joseph Merinyo, its president and an entrepreneur of far-ranging activities. He was the primary target of a campaign which exposed the seamier side of colonial rule in Tanganyika. Once the administration involved C. C. Monckton in coffee marketing, a significant network developed on the mountain. An expatriate named J. P. Molloy managed the Moshi branch of C. C. Monckton from February 1928 to March 1931. During this time he and Merinyo worked together in marketing the coffee which KNPA members chose to sell through the Association.[11] The bureaucracy uncovered evidence of their alleged collusion to defraud KNPA members. This conspiracy purportedly consisted of short-weighing coffee and deducting too much for the receptacles in which coffee was brought.

While the administration detected collusion on the mountain, including the man who audited the KNPA accounts,[12] legal charges intersected with political necessities in the subsequent adjudication. Examination of evidence brought against Molloy and Merinyo is impossible, because material available to the court was not accessible to the author. The court acquitted Molloy on the charges of stealing coffee. It exonerated Merinyo of all but one offense; for supposedly stealing Shillings 420/22 he received a sentence of six months simple imprisonment.

Whatever the facts,[13] more than a search for justice motivated the proceedings. Molloy apparently engaged in activities besides managing the Moshi branch of C. C. Monckton. Provincial Commissioner G. F. Webster, Northern, described him as a "bad influence," one "inclined to incite natives to political agitation."[14] There was a strong connection between the bureaucracy's decision to prosecute Merinyo and the KNPA's willingness to keep him as president. Webster cabled the Secretariat on July 4, 1931, that "despite exposure thefts majority at meeting wish to retain Joseph as President." He added, "Propose to prosecute."[15] Webster hoped the allegations would suffice to remove Merinyo, so prosecution was an escalation in the plan to sack him. Just how determined officers were appears in another confidential dispatch from Webster to the Secretariat, August 25, 1931. Webster doubted Merinyo would be convicted on the "larger question of short-weighing," and in this he was prescient. But it "was essential to discredit Merinyo." Webster wrote, "We used Chagga agents and counter-propaganda." Joseph Maliti, who succeeded Merinyo by bureaucratic intervention as the new president of the KNPA, "spearheaded the D. O.'s propaganda."[16]

In the midst of this intrigue, the central question was, Why did the bureaucracy want to remove Merinyo? The answer was straightforward. Webster reported that the Chagga chiefs were pleased that Merinyo's power and that of his friends was broken. Their pleasure was matched by the bureaucracy's relief. One chief, quoted by Webster, expressed the cardinal fact, "These people's influence is over the whole tribe whereas our influence is only in our own sections of the mountain."[17] But a less threatening president was only a cosmetic change. The administration knew that a fundamental revision in structure was imperative.

This revision, which transformed the KNPA into the Kilimanjaro Native Co-operative Union (KNCU), was delicate.[18] A primary objective was to work for an optimal level of subtribal localism and fragmentation. The controlling principle was "to build up an organization around the Chiefs . . . we must therefore do nothing which will weaken the Chiefs' power or prestige."[19] Because traditional power was diffused throughout many chiefdoms and subchiefdoms, the bureaucracy had to devise an analogue in cooperative organization which reflected that configuration. The KNPA was, of course, a local organization. But it was one that had promoted district-wide horizontal economic integration because of its unitary structure. The KNPA also suggested the potential of transethnic combination because some members were not Chagga. Administrators did consider whether the new organization should be one district-wide society or a central union with separate divisions. They chose, as no surprise, the confederal option and made vertical ties between the center and divisions loose.

In one sense, reorganization was reactionary: rejuvenating very local units restored aspects of the *status quo ante* KNPA. In another sense, revision was conservative: it attempted to preserve a district-wide element through a central union, although the KNCU was to be largely a tribal association of Chagga. The actual process of reorganization showed that key parties on all sides knew what was happening. Secretary of Native Affairs Mitchell ordered the drafting of one set of byelaws for the sectional societies, another for the union. To a suspicious committee of the KNPA he emphasized that the union was really "the dominant body." This assertion found some support on a paper table of organization. But when the KNPA committee pleaded for one president of the new union, trying to preserve a strong postion at the top, Mitchell responded with a semantic nonchalance that shows that the connection between location of power and gradation of title had changed during reorganization. He said it was "no problem" to designate that position as "president" since the heads of the local societies were called "chairmen."[20]

EXTENDING THE REGULATORY WEB: THE "CHAGGA RULE"

Once the KNCU was legally in place, the bureaucracy pursued a kind of vertical regulation in the north after 1932 which fewer and fewer Chagga coffee growers could avoid. This compulsion expanded to include crucial aspects of production and distribution. Both the manner and timing of this pursuit, more than any other factors, catalyzed unrest in forms which the administration could understand. Under the embryonic KNCU, members retained that freedom from KNPA days to sell wherever and to whomever they pleased. However, this apparent independence was more and more affected by government decisions restricting the number of coffee buyers who could operate in the Moshi district. Nonetheless, the web of compulsion was not yet unbreakable. And people, upset with the management of the union or with its structure, possessed a liberty which most of the time acted as a safety valve and prevented unrest from escalating into overt protest. But the bureaucracy removed the individual's right to sell as he pleased when it enacted the so-called "Chagga Rule" in 1934. The rule prescribed that every African in the Moshi district market his coffee through the KNCU.

The "Chagga Rule" originated in the special mixture of finance and law which gave British administration in Tanganyika its characteristic flavor. The savings which can result from economies of size in bulk marketing became evident to the Secretariat. And bulk marketing, it was thought, might give the KNCU increased bargaining power in the international coffee market. In seeking those advantages, administrators decided to make the union a monopsonist in relation to the individual grower. But difficulties arose in giving the KNCU's position as sole buyer legal expression.

After all the discussion and drafting that went into the general Cooperative Societies Ordinance of 1932,[21] the bureaucracy found it ill suited to handle this specific problem. That legislation was not, the law officers advised, a proper vehicle for implementing the compulsory sales necessary to maximize bulk marketing. So the administration fell back on

Section 15 of the Native Authority Ordinance (1923), which gave those Authorities the power, subject to the Governor's approval, to make rules concerning peace, order, and welfare. Section 15's elasticity of interpretation was the foundation for the "Chagga Rule." The bureaucracy repeated the mode of enforcement it had used in implementing the Coffee Industry (Registration and Improvement) Ordinance of 1928: the Native Authorities were to act as local enforcers. Indirect rule politics thus became entangled with the cooperative society, whose functions the administration claimed were economic and financial but which in practice meshed with life on the mountain.

This partial intersection of a Native Authority with a cooperative society unified politics and economics, defined in the bureaucracy's own terms, and created an arena of political economy. This arena became a forum of two-way communication. The more realistic the arena and forum, the greater was the danger for the bureaucracy; colonialism thrives on preserving the fragmented identities of its dependents, distorted descriptions of power relationships, and disharmonies among the levels of communication. Needless to say, the bureaucracy did not set out to create this particular arena and forum. Lambert emphasized that the arrangement was "makeshift," since it facilitated involvement of the Native Authorities in the affairs of the KNCU and so brought the union into the field of politics.[22] Enactment of the "Chagga Rule" opened the way for a particular combination of legal and physical protests that exposed the vulnerability of the Tanganyika bureaucracy.

The "Chagga Rule" also brought the Native Authorities into the field of economics and created new problems for them. Changes in the economic sphere, such as price declines for coffee and attendant debates over what the union should pay to growers, could now affect their fortunes. The outcome was makeshift, because the stability of the bureaucracy's local surrogates depended directly upon forces which these Authorities could not control. Destabilization would affect more than one administrative level. If adverse economic changes buffeted the Native Authorities, the Tanganyika administration would be threatened.

These exogenous changes did occur. The initial one was a downswing in the price which Moshi coffee obtained in the international market, a decline not related to deterioration in quality. But price fluctuations interlocked with other factors to produce a 1930s profile reported in table 8.1, which uses government figures on prices and tonnage to compute gross receipts. The two key seasons for gross receipts reductions were 1934–1935 and, precipitously, 1936–1937. The first occurred against a background of falling prices but rising output; the second in an environment of mildly recovering prices but significantly reduced tonnage. The

TABLE 8.1.
GROSS "NATIVE" COFFEE RECEIPTS FROM 1932 THROUGH 1938 (MOSHI)

Season	Price in Pounds per Ton			Tonnage	Gross Receipts (Pounds)
1932–3	38	1	7d.*	1,070	40,744.708
1933–4	35			1,168	40,880.
1934–5	22	17	2d.	1,595	36,445.75
1935–6	23	7	7d.	1,791	41,872.086
1936–7	27	15		881	24,447.75
1937–8	28	1		1,400 (est.)	39,270.

Note: These are seasonal average prices realized for parchment coffee in new bags, free on rail at Moshi station, with coffee tax paid.
Source: *Report of the Department of Agriculture for 1937* (Dar es Salaam, 1938), 2:26.
*Pence

extent that greater productivity or expansion of existing coffee shambas [plots] or the increasing number of growers account for rising output in the first season of income reduction is not known. But the second and more dramatic decline in receipts, resulting largely from a halving of output, took place during a season of intense unrest on the mountain. The timing here is more than coincidental. The fact that coffee prices plummeted and receipts declined during the initial season of the "Chagga Rule" did not bode well for the stability of colonial institutions.

Some producers began their analysis of price fluctuations with the structure of the KNCU, the institution which affected their livelihoods most directly, and fastened on its monopsonistic character. This target was inviting, because it exhibited the union's major internal contradiction. The "Chagga Rule" had completed the negation of voluntariness. Some officers admitted the contradiction for a cooperative society but argued that special circumstances legitimized the monopsony. These pertained to those economies of bulk marketing but now included the three-fourths rule, contained in Section 36 of Ordinance 7 of 1932 (Co-operative Societies [Amendment][23] Ordinance). If a cooperative society enlisted more than 75 percent of all producers who accounted for at least 75 percent of total output, then it could register every producer and market all output in an area regardless of the wishes of a minority.

A minority did think it could get a better price for its coffee on the open market by avoiding the overhead costs of the KNCU. This belief rested to some extent on individual entrepreneurial confidence but gained strength from a suspicion that the KNCU was shielding itself from the full impact of price declines by passing on harm disproportionately to member growers. There was some basis for this conviction, because the KNCU followed a bureaucratic canon that when retrenchment is necessary, the last item cut is internal structure. Allowing harm to fall more on growers than on staff violated a purpose of a cooperative society: to smooth out the impact of price fluctuations on all members. Whether the KNCU acted equitably in sorting out the effects of price reductions is not known, but a significant and articulate minority thought not. And this dissatisfaction propelled them to take action.

ORCHESTRATING GRIEVANCES

Some of the dissatisfied minority turned to the British legal system. Five Africans of the Moshi district filed five suits in the Tanganyika High Court against the Native Authorities and the KNCU. The common objective of these suits was to have the "Chagga Rule" declared invalid. The legal proceedings lasted several years and their cadence determined, in part, the intensity of other protests. The initial phase of this court action prodded administrators to tackle coffee marketing directly rather than through the Native Authority Ordinance. If the "Chagga Rule" were overturned, new machinery "to provide for the sanitation and marketing of native grown coffee was essential."[24] The bureaucracy prepared legislation for all African coffee, not just Chagga coffee. Thus it reverted to its basic quasi-legal administrative approach, which put objectives couched in very generalized language into the forms of specific legal ordinances.

As the High Court pondered the issues which the Chagga suits raised throughout 1936, the pace of activity in the north accelerated. How many became protesters, and if they ever became a majority, are unanswerable questions. But the weight of testimonial evidence suggests that filing law suits activated more and more people in the protest. "Discontent became general and a number of secret meetings were arranged by the malcontents in the Machame Chiefdom at which open sedition was preached and plans made for overt acts of violence against constituted authority."[25] The word "general" in Lambert's account is ambiguous; whether discontent became general throughout Machame or spread over the mountain is unclear. In any event, the Court of the Chagga Council convicted four ringleaders of attending unauthorized meetings and of conduct calculated to bring the authority of the Chief and the Native Administration into contempt.

At the same time, the central administration was trying to get more information on coffee growing and its impact on Chagga society. R. C. Northcote developed figures (shown in table 8.2) which distinguished growers in groups based on the number of trees each person controlled. These facts showed that coffee growing had, for about 1675 people or 8 percent of the KNCU's membership, advanced beyond the 1000-tree

TABLE 8.2.
CHAGGA COFFEE GROWERS DIFFERENTIATED

Trees	Members	Percentage
1–500	16,074	74
501–1000	3,988	18
1001–1500	1,082	5
1501–2000	292	1.5
2001 and over	301	1.5
Total	21,737	100.0

Source: CO 691/156/42117. Extract from Northcote's confidential letter to the Chief Secretary, Dar, on the KNCU, March 1936.

limit associated with peasant cultivation in the 1920s.[26] Administrators knew that coffee was a source of new money and thereby of a power independent of Native Administration, but now realized just how vigorously some were pursuing this enterprise. Yet not everything fit into their terms, and this incongruence made officials nervous. Northcote reported, "The Chagga have neither the conception of shares, in the European sense of the word, nor of a dividend on shares, nor do they appreciate that shares serve as security for outsiders' claims. . . . They feel they have a right or part in [the KNCU] as a group, and not a share valued in terms of money."[27]

In September 1937, the High Court dismissed the "Chagga Rule" suits on the technical ground that plaintiffs did not have a right to initiate them. The Court finessed the substantive issue—the validity of the rule itself. The decision followed the 1936 events in the Machame Chiefdom, which resulted in the imprisonment of two principal leaders, Daudi Ngamini and Asari Ephraim. Chagga justice, administered by the chiefs and backed by British military power, dealt with its local problem. But when the High Court rejected the suits without ruling on the central issue, dissatisfaction with formal British justice heightened a feeling that the bureaucracy was employing tribal law to repress dissenters. The target in 1936 seemed to be the Native Administration; in 1937 it moved and the KNCU came to the fore. This shift was not total. The mode of enforcing the "Chagga Rule," indeed its origin, had made both the Native Administration and the KNCU seem but two faces of an oppressive bureaucratic Janus.

On September 15 a group of people in Machame interfered with the daily routine of the KNCU's staff there. These intruders threatened some employees and physically obstructed others. About 200 people closed three union stores by force, demolished them, and smashed up the coffee-weighing apparatus. On the morning of September 18, three days later, about 2,000 people wrecked the union's coffee storage shed and destroyed the weighing machinery at Marangu East. These indisputable breaches of the colonial public peace moved the administration to preserve its version of law and order in the territory. Police reinforcements went to the district, and two Royal Air Force planes from Nairobi reasserted the colonial presence.[28] Suppressed and terrorized, the disturbers of the peace stopped the physical expression of their dissatisfaction.

This military response represented considerable force in its context and reflected a deep concern for the explosive potential of the so-called "coffee riots." But in both their private and public explanations, Tanganyika administrators reported measurements of significance conveying minimization: the violence was minor; the numbers involved small; the dissatisfaction did not mirror the "true feelings" of the vast majority of Chagga. Acting Governor D. W. Kennedy stated the official line to Colonial Secretary W. G. A. Ormsby-Gore, September 27, 1937, "The agitation against the K.N.C.U. was fomented and instigated by a comparatively small number of malcontents, [and] was directed solely against the K.N.C.U."[29] An official memorandum on the riots scored "agitators, mostly ex-officials of the old K.N.P.A.," who capitalized on disappointment among growers "engendered by the non-payment of a final dividend." It also blamed those who lost out on the profitable lorry trade when collecting centers were established in every area and transport provided by the KNCU.[30]

Some in the Colonial Office saw through the language of minimization. F. Lee studied Kennedy's letter and concluded, "From the fact that the agitators succeeded in getting a fairly large following (at least in Machame Central) and from the fact that the disturbances also occurred at Marangu, one suspects that the original discontent was much more widespread than the Tanganyika Authorities believed."[31] Although Lee was right, an appraisal of the significance of protest cannot be based entirely on crowd size, damage done, or repressive forces required. These riots were only a military intermezzo in a symphony of protest. The most dangerous area for the administration was judicial, and proceedings became more intricate.

When the High Court in Tanganyika dismissed the "Chagga Rule" suits, plaintiffs decided to appeal the ruling to the Appeals Court in Nairobi. The suit was reinstituted, but the Dar es Salaam bureaucracy refused to contest the appeal. Some officials in Tanganyika and London downplayed the importance of subsequent court proceedings. Lambert, for instance, thought in 1939 the result only "of academic interest," since the administration had taken control over the coffee industry directly and the "Chagga Rule" had been cancelled by the chiefs.[32] But these cases held far more than "academic interest." They raised difficult questions about relations between the bureaucracy and its Native Authorities. They exposed the inherent vulnerability of quasi-legal colonial administration to a well-designed legal challenge from within. And they exemplified a strategy that became more important in Tanganyika in the 1950s—using higher levels of a system to attack lower ones and, when extended, international agencies to pressure national governments and territorial administrations.

Why did the Tanganyika bureaucracy not contest the appeal? The answer lies in the rationale for the High Court's dismissal of the original suits. Plaintiffs did not have power to file, according to the High Court, because Native Authorities were agents of government, protected by the doctrine of sovereign immunity from suits filed against them without their consent. In its initial ruling, the High Court had given the bureaucracy a temporary edge, but this advantage carried an excessive maintenance cost. Had administrators supported the High Court's ruling in the appeals proceedings in Nairobi, they would have conceded that Native Administration was an inseparable level of colonial government.

Once again the quasi-legal dilemma intruded. J. H. Vaughan, Tanganyika's Solicitor General, contended, "The Chagga Council [of Chiefs] should be regarded in law as an integral part of the machinery of Government—at any rate it may be argued that they were acting as *agents of Government* in so far as they were carrying out a policy at the dictation of Government."[33] But Governor MacMichael had decided, "It would be most inadvisable to attempt to support the judgment of the High Court which, in placing native authorities in the same position as departments of State, gave them a status never contemplated when the system of local government was set up."[34] Vaughan suspected that Acting Governor Kennedy regarded the Native Authority "as an independent statutory body somewhat analogous to a local Government body in England." Vaughan noted, "This uncertainty as to the status of the Native Authorities must be reflected, to some extent, in any answer to the question as to the validity of their bye-laws." An ambiguous relationship between Native Administration and higher levels of bureaucracy was a basis for stability in this context. Law would define the leash precisely; the administration wanted its existence certified, though its length kept indeterminate.

But not specifying the length of the leash might alter the definition of the tethered and ambiguous ties might become precarious. Such a transition began when the East African Court of Appeals reversed the High Court judgment. In July 1938, the original issue—the validity of the "Chagga Rule"—was still sub judice, having been sent back to the High Court. The Appeals Court ruled, "Government cannot be properly

joined as a defendant," given the administration's refusal to contest.
This decision led to another irony of quasi-legal colonial rule. The law officers were still representing the Native Authorities, because as the
Secretariat noted, "The rule which is being challenged could not have
been effective without the approval of the Governor."[35] But the main
thrust of the Appeals Court's judgment established that the Council of
Chiefs and the Native Authorities did not possess the immunities or
privileges of a department of state. The Court had decided what the
Chagga Council and Native Authorities lacked but did not indicate what
powers these bodies did possess. This act of exclusion, not counter-
balanced by one of attribution, destabilized administrative structures.[36]

Meanwhile, administrators were redeploying their control techniques. They established a Native Coffee Board in the Moshi district
under provisions of the Native Produce Coffee (Control and Marketing)
Ordinance of 1937. Thus administrators disentangled their different
types of indirect rule—political through Native Authorities and economic
through cooperatives. The composition of this Coffee Board gave equal
seats to Moshi residents and British bureaucrats but not an equal say. At
their first meeting on November 23, 1937, members unanimously asked
the Governor and Legislative Council to sanction the KNCU as marketing
agent of the Board. This meant all producers of "native" coffee in the
Moshi district could sell only to the KNCU.[37]

The administration was taking a safer route to monopsony this time.
The Board from which this request emanated had four members, two
officials and two Africans. The chairman was W. S. Yates, who was also
the acting district officer. Elected secretary under Rule 4(3) was J. R.
Curry, the agricultural officer. The two "native" representatives were
William bin Mbatia and Ndaskoi bin Matinga. Neither held any special
post on the Coffee Board. Because the bureaucracy monopolized both
gavel and records, the genuineness of the "unanimous" request for
monopsony cannot be determined. But key positions showed what was
happening. If the Native Authorities failed, then a four-member committee, stage-managed from within, might succeed.

The Native Authorities performed one more controversial act of entanglement. The bureaucracy wanted to get rid of the "Chagga Rule."
Its original crude attempt at monopsony was proving embarrassing.
London, as well as some Tanganyika officials, preferred that the rule
"unobtrusively lapse."[38] But the "Chagga Rule" did not fade away; the
chiefs cancelled it and thereby fueled controversy again. To withdraw
itself from the KNCU, the Native Authority asserted a right to cancel the
rule. Action thus proceeded on debatable logical and legal grounds.
With no right to initiate, there is no right to cancel. Whether proper or

not, cancellation rendered any High Court decision on the original substantive issue moot. But it did not remove a destabilizing ambiguity now enshrouding the relationship between Native Authorities and the central administration.

Most Tanganyika officials knew they had a serious problem. Yet their perceptions of both the size and meaning of the 1937 disturbances remained selective and superficial. They underrated the damage Chagga litigation had inflicted on the fragile foundations of quasi-legal colonial administration. In the Colonial Office H. Cruttwell noted on April 22, 1938, that a district officer, who had recently toured the area, endorsed the newspapers' assertion: there was more discontent beneath the surface than high Tanganyika officials cared to admit. Those officials discounted that report on grounds of the tour's brevity and the officer's lack of local experience. They preferred the view of Bishop Byrne, Roman Catholic Bishop of Moshi, that discontent was limited to a very small number of people.[39]

PAYING THE PRICE

Although officials minimized the extent of participation, they took no chances with those found most active. The Governor signed deportation orders for at least thirteen people, based partly on sworn statements submitted by forty-nine Africans in the Moshi district "which showed that these ringleaders had been inciting members of the Chagga tribe to hold secret meetings in defiance of the Chiefs' orders."[40] Messrs. Atkinson, Bown, Morrison, and Ainsley, the legal firm representing these Chagga, petitioned the Secretary of State for an independent inquiry into the deportations.[41] An investigation was never held, but the petition contains the identities of those deported and indicates why the bureaucracy regarded the cases as "extreme."[42] The deportees represented a diverse coalition that invalidates any monochromatic analysis of the northern unrest. Their profiles[43] show that local and sometimes familial grievances against certain chiefs moved some to participate; dissatisfaction with the KNCU motivated others; some had interlocking complaints; and a segment of the coalition drew on coffee money to support the legal battle against the "Chagga Rule."

The deportees were drawn from participants in every phase of the unrest. Daudi Ngamini, Asser Ephraim, and Topia Masaki were all arrested in June 1936, tried by the Chagga Native Council, sentenced to six months in jail for alleged illegal assembly, then deported at the expiration of their prison sentences. Ngamini's career illustrates a rich blend of grievances. He was a cousin of then chief of Mashame Hery Abdiel Shangali[44] and had "a long standing dispute with Hery Abdiel as to his inheritance." His dispute entered the arena of bureaucratic politics through the offices of the KNCU. "In November, 1935, when there was dissatisfaction with the K.N.C.U. he was elected chairman of the subsidiary society of Mashame Central. This election was quashed by Captain Hallier the P. C. Arusha as being illegal in December, 1935." Ngamini had temporarily achieved a power base that might have rivaled his cousin's. But Hallier's rejection removed that possibility and intensified Ngamini's opposition to official meddling in local affairs.

The second member of this trio was Asser Ephraim, a teacher whose skills became important to the members of the subsidiary society of Mashame Central. He was appointed in 1935 "to take correct minutes of the meetings to prevent their being misreported by the chief." He "also allowed his typewriter to be used for various letters and petitions to the Provincial Commissioner." In April and May 1936, he joined in giving instructions to Mr. Baker Smith, their advocate, and helped collect legal fees. He was then arrested, sentenced, and deported. The third member was Topia Masaki, described as an "elderly teacher much respected." In September 1937, Acting Governor Kennedy called Masaki "the leader of the agitation" and portrayed him as a "dismissed mission teacher who was sentenced to six months in jail for holding an unauthorized meeting."[45] Masaki had a dispute with Chief Hery Abdiel over a sum of seventy shillings, "which he deposited, as ordered, to pay compensation for possible injury to crops by a road which he had made. The Chief neither paid over any compensation for damage to crops nor returned the money in spite of frequent demands." Masaki and Ngamini thus were disputing with Chief Abdiel for different reasons, but both grievances went beyond personal and business relationships. Ngamini and Ephraim were key figures in the local section of the KNCU, though the secretary lasted longer than the chairman.

The other deportees were involved at various stages of the activity. The fourth deportee was N. Gadi Msue, an elder of the Chiefs Council. Msue was one of the plaintiffs in the High Court cases. "This is the sole reason for his deportation in October, 1937." The bureaucracy did not respond to the particulars of the petition here. And it is not clear whether the police ever located Msue to deport him. The fifth deportee was Toma Bin Mafalu, a mason of Mashame East. He had a personal grievance against Chief Abdiel, having worked for him and allegedly not received payment. He became one of the plaintiffs representing Mashame East, was arrested in September 1937, and was subsequently deported. The fourth and fifth deportees were thus visible as plaintiffs in the Chagga cases. Fostering Mafalu's involvement was a grievance against Chief Abdiel, a thread which unites several deportees. But he was also protesting what Abdiel had come to represent.

The sixth deportee was Joshua Mwashuka, a coffee cultivator of Mashame Central. "He was signatory to a letter drawn by Mr. Baker Smith resigning from the subsidiary society in October, 1936." His resignation was a protest against the "Chagga Rule." This motivation was central to his departure, because he collected fees for the continued prosecution of the Chagga cases. He was deported in September 1937. The seventh deportee was Mose Kirenga, a carpenter with a coffee shamba in Mashame East. His involvement seems based on the twin prongs of dissatisfaction with the local chief and the "Chagga Rule." Kirenga had worked for Abdiel and allegedly not received payment. He had signed the letter of resignation from the Mashame East Co-operative Society. He "assisted in giving instructions to Mr. Baker Smith and in collecting fees for the case." He also was deported in September 1937. The case of the eighth deportee is more complicated. Anderson Ananduni was a tailor with a coffee shamba but was also a Native Authority clerk collecting the hut tax. "A deficiency occurred and according to our information Anderson was made the scapegoat and punished instead of the guilty superior." No evidence corroborates this point. Whatever the facts of Ananduni's behavior as a tax collector, he did also collect legal fees for the Chagga cases. He was arrested in June 1938, near Moshi, when he was with his advocate Mr. Morrison.

A sketch of the ninth deportee shows how perceptions of the inequitable functioning of the KNCU could actuate participation in the protest. Samuel Nderingo was a mason with a coffee shamba at Marangu. He was "elected in July, 1936, to consult Mr. Baker Smith when trouble arose over the balance ('baki') and went to Arusha for that purpose." He became one of the plaintiffs and resigned from the local Co-operative Society. He was arrested and deported in June 1938. Kimatare Seuta, the tenth deportee, was a trader with a coffee shamba at Marangu. He signed the letter of resignation from the local Co-operative Association and collected legal fees for the court cases. He was arrested and sentenced to six months in jail by the Mangi of Kibosho in January 1937, and again arrested, and deported, in September 1937. The eleventh and twelfth deportees, Israel Mtunga and Anasa Masika, were coffee cultivators at Marangu. Both joined in giving instructions to Mr. Baker Smith and in collecting fees for the court cases. Both were deported in October 1937. The thirteenth deportee, Toudor, was a coffee cultivator of Kibosho. He was not active in Mr. Baker Smith's time, but did give instructions to Mr. Webster and "was particularly active in arranging for the costs of the appeal in spite of the strong opposition of the chief.'' In September 1937, ''in order to avoid victimisation he left Kibosho.'' In April 1938, he was deported.

The profile of the fourteenth and last deportee demonstrates the entanglement of Native Administration with the KNCU and how opposition to one could become resistance to the other. Leonardi cultivated a ''considerable coffee shamba at Kibosho.'' At a meeting ''in connection with the K.N.C.U. announcement in or about May, 1936 that the 'baki' was 3 cents a pound only he was a prominent spokesman and for this he was sentenced by the chief to six months imprisonment.'' Whether his sentence was the result only of complaints about the size of the coffee ''baki'' is difficult to ascertain. If petitioners' inferences are correct, the chief was using his power to repress opposition to the management of the KNCU.

The petition describes two other men who were not deported. Bernardi Kiwera was a cultivator with a large coffee shamba at Kibosho and a plaintiff in the High Court cases.[46] In or about May 1936, ''at a meeting with reference to the 'baki' of 3 cents a pound only he spoke complaining of the absence of any accounts of explanation as to how the balance was so little. For this reason he was sentenced by the chief to six months imprisonment.'' After his release, Kiwera consulted Mr. Baker Smith and became a plaintiff in the court cases. When the Appeals Court reinstated the Chagga cases, he circulated a translation of the ruling. This decision ''was in such technical terms that there were no doubt several mistakes in the translation. According to our instructions it was for this reason that the Chagga Council sentenced him to six months imprisonment for fitina (i.e. agitation, intrigue, sedition) in April, 1938.'' The second nondeportee was Hans Ebenezer Reuben, the son of a subchief of Mashame, and another plaintiff. ''He has a considerable coffee plantation and two shops and is of good education. Since 1936 he has been a voluntary exile from his home as he is under the belief, which we are satisfied is absolutely genuine that if he returns to Mashame some false charge will be trumped up against him and he will be arrested or deported.''

SUMMARIZING SIGNIFICANCE

These sixteen individuals constituted a diverse leadership coalition among the Chagga. Some were teachers, some were coffee cultivators, some combined masonry with coffee growing, and so on. To call some of these men peasants or small-scale growers is accurate; Mtunga and Masika may have fit that category. But other men controlled some of the considerable coffee plantations shown in Northcote's table (table 8.2). This leadership coalition was neither stratified in its membership nor alienated from the aspirations of many Chagga. People with multiple grievances and various backgrounds not only made up the leadership but its increasing support as well. Many backed the coalition by contributing money for the legal cases.[47] The protesters' ability to locate and expose weaknesses in the colonial control apparatus upset its managers, so they deported the leadership to then remote parts of the territory.[48] But deportation was an early admission of an inability to co-opt people who, as G. Bushe in the Colonial Office put it, had "some education."[49] As communications improved and mobility increased, deportation could not stifle the subversive threat which similar coalitions with more territorial goals and global publicity represented.

How did the Tanganyika administration fare with this serious interwar challenge to its structures? On the riot field, of course, it won, and the protesters lost. But the military entr'acte was the least significant phase. Using the metropolitan court system against the territorial bureaucracy—and winning—revealed the vulnerability of quasi-legal colonial administration to defeat by having British standards of justice applied to its own actions. The strategy of playing one part of a system against another, which worked so well for some Chagga, would return again and again in different variations as the territorial independence movement gained strength in the 1950s.

The warning from the mountain echoed ominously and spoke differently to various interests, but it spoke with one voice to the intermediate and highest levels of British government—as a complicated portent.

9

Retrospective and Comparative Agenda

"The governing principle should be to adapt the machinery of administration to fit the actual conditions of trade and not attempt to canalize trade soastofacilitatethetaskofadministration."

—Colonial Secretary P. Cunliffe-Lister, *commenting on amended versions of three Tanganyika ordinances dealing with trade and markets, May 2, 1932.*

W H E N Phillip Cunliffe-Lister wrote the above injunction, which is repeated from chapter 3, he penned a most succinct warning against what the Tanganyika bureaucracy was doing to economic life within the territory. "To facilitate the task of administration," Tanganyika officials were not only "canalizing" trade but also manipulating most other aspects of economic activity. Their endeavors produced a version of economy that should no longer be classified as simply intermediate. Tanganyika's bureaucratic economy rested on a distinctive calculus of maximization and minimization, operated in ways that sometimes conflicted with what others desired, and had acquired a regulatory momentum of its own.

In previous pages I have shown that bureaucratic economy in action, especially its impact on individual people. And I have examined how some Tanganyikans protested increasing government intervention in their lives with checkered consequences for themselves and the territorial administration. I will now summarize the harmful consequences of bureaucratic action that can be analyzed as internally generated forms of underdevelopment. The following résumé neither ranks nor completely separates what are often interwoven harms.

Extraction as excessive self-servicing. Most students of underdevelopment concentrate on extraction as a process of external removal of resources from a territory on unequal or inequitable terms. While this focus is legitimate, it should not remain exclusive, since most of what the bureaucratic economy extracted went for administrative self-maintenance and expansion. A reinvestment of extraction so geared was both a major general form and source of underdevelopment. The bureaucratic economy became too powerful in relation to more microeconomic kinds of community, group, and personal action within the territory; this imbalance is a crucial form of underdevelopment. And the bureaucratic economy was itself a primary perpetrator of more specific forms of underdevelopment such as distorted exchange articulation, market articulation, factor allocation, and economic communication.

Distorted exchange articulation. Extraction, especially indirect taxes and railroad rates, hampered exchange, reduced the territory's capacities as importer and exporter, and constrained Tanganyika's international economic relationships. The administration's definitions of trade and traders, its trade licensing schedule, and its restrictive credit and collateral policies all frustrated the emergence of peer economic relations within Tanganyika. The two reinforcing results of those administrative actions— the entrenchment of economic inequity and the enlargement of dependent opportunity—are among the most important kinds of exchange disarticulation.

Distorted market articulation. The bureaucratic economy distorted the aggregation of exchange in several ways. Positioning official markets more on financial than economic criteria surely qualifies as a gross dislocation of activity. And the suppression of a grass-roots kind of horizontal economic integration constitutes perhaps the most significant general harm in this area. Administrative action distorted the emergence of some kinds of markets, such as those for agricultural produce. It stifled the growth of other types, such as territorial credit and money markets broadly defined.[1] Probably most consequential for the people of Tanganyika in the short run was the disarticulation of various levels of local food markets serving internal needs.

Distorted factor allocation. Had there been no administrative barriers hampering the emergence of a multitiered, horizontally integrated territorial food market, many Tanganyikans would still have had the anterior problem of producing food to exchange. Bureaucratic pressure on local production decisions was highlighted in the discussion of the "plant-more-crops" campaign. It led farmers in too many locations to misallocate their factors of production in ways that undercut their own food-producing capacities. While I stressed distorted uses of land and labor in chapter 6, there is no doubt in my mind that administrative manipulation produced a misallocation of entrepreneurial ability, the economist's fourth conventional factor of production.

This distortion occurred not only in agriculture, but also in commerce. That so many African traders were on the lowest occupational rungs of the trading profession as small-scale, small-time business people, which was partly a consequence of the entrenchment of economic inequity, also represents an overallocation of skills to those job categories. If one construes that fourth factor in its widest sense as actual and potential managerial ability or skill, the kinds of tasks which Native Administration offered some Tanganyikans involved more distortion. Those with any degree of managerial ability or promise usually found their skill and potential underutilized and its allocation thereby distorted. So the misallocation of factors characterized administration itself.

Distorted economic communication. The language and mechanisms of economic communication received special administrative abuse.[2] The damage inflicted on the price mechanism and the confusion which resulted from mixing markets of prices with those of pressures are especially insidious. This damage and confusion further distorted factor allocation and disarticulated exchange and its aggregation. These interwoven harms constitute much of the historical record and legacy of Tanganyika's bureaucratic economy.

The significance of this case study also resides in its more general contexts. When one investigates a range of published and unpublished documents, including sometimes neglected inside sources, one finds that the realities of the colonial bureaucratic presence, at least in the case of inter-war Tanganyika, are too complex for slotting in any existing paradigm that features Africa's incorporation into an international economic order.

To accept as either accurate or complete for all cases Professor Immanuel Wallerstein's description of the two main functions colonial bureaucracies had during his second phase (1900–1975) of Africa's involvement in the "world-economy" is no longer possible in light of the Tanganyika experience. According to Wallerstein, one of the most prominent and imaginative of the systems-builders working today, colonial administrations had "to construct the necessary economic infrastructure. This was done more or less on a cost basis. The taxes on African direct producers largely covered the costs of this infrastructure, but it brought in no profit as such. . . ." Their second function was "to assure a proper location of African producers" in order to satisfy the direct and derived demands of production for a "world market."[3] This assessment is not even correct in a preliminary sense for the Tanganyika situation. It glosses over the frequent Tanganyika Railroad administration deficits that not even high freight rates covered. It falsely assumes that Tanganyika bureaucrats had the kinds of knowledge about local economic conditions and the desire to fine-tune location of producers with the types and levels of commodity production appropriate for that ill-specified "world market."

Nor do the Tanganyika facts justify acceptance of the more regional, East African pattern advanced by Professor E. A. Brett. Colonial bureaucracy was, he grants, "a primary agent in the creation of the contemporary state of underdevelopment in East Africa." But then he qualifies agency in this sense: as a reinforcer or insurer of the "dominance of imported capital and skills and hence continued dependence on the outside world."[4]

That argument falls far short of capturing the multiple modes of underdevelopment associated with the entrenchment of Tanganyika's bureaucratic economy. Nor, in view of the Tanganyika evidence, can one fully endorse the kind of congruence he cites "between the interests of a bureaucracy committed to large-scale centralized administrative structures for reasons of simplicity of management and economy and those of private producing and trading groups that needed to have services provided at the *cheapest possible rate.*"[5] (My italics added.) So the Tanganyika case does undermine the validity of explaining all origins of underdevelopment everywhere by remaining only within the prevalent macroeconomic categories which now seem inappropriately formulated and generalized.

I strongly suspect that more detailed research on other territorial colonial bureaucracies will enrich our sense of complexity in still other ways and perhaps even salvage some combination of insights from the wreckage of now overconceptualized "world-systems." Gaining more refined knowledge concerning the zones of convergence and divergence may help define further the transformation theme so vital to understanding the significance of colonial bureaucracies and so pivotal for writing the histories of underdevelopment and African government bureaucracy in a related, deliberate fashion.

The European penetration of Africa was a complicated process that eventually involved a seemingly straightforward *transfer* of "western-type bureaucracy" as colonial administrations established themselves on the continent. But these institutions underwent multiple *transformations* over time, as their managers evolved, for instance, modes of control and extraction. While reinforcing objectives held by some, these modes diverged in important ways from what others wanted.

Readers have witnessed these zones of convergence and divergence for pre-1941 Tanganyika. Illuminating them for other administrations must be done on a case-by-case basis. It must rest on a solid foundation of research into each bureaucracy's past internal records. It must take into account how and to what extent each institution organized relationships of production, distribution, and exchange to meet its particular requirements for revenue and stability.

Of course, scholars must continue to probe Africa's international economic relationships—their origins, evolution, and local mutations. But future research on all facets of underdevelopment should look more at relationships on every level of aggregation—between and among individual persons, between and among the groups and classes to which people may or may not belong, and between and among economic groupings that may or may not qualify as economies. In short, the targeting of research must exhibit more pinpoint precision if we wish to obtain a priority sense of which specific relationships caused the greatest harm and of those which may be most amenable or vulnerable to change.

The gaps in historical knowledge that prevent the crystallization of an accurate sense of priority are not the kinds scholars can afford to fill at their leisure. Territorial colonial bureaucracies were—and as the institutional ancestors of legally independent African administrations, still are—a major source of some forms of the underdevelopment that afflicts Africa today. The tenacity of past crippling structures remaining in some liberated governments significantly retards the capacities of large numbers of Africans to improve their economic welfare, which for many may mean achieving only minimal standards of nutrition, health, and opportunity.

APPENDIX

IMPERIAL ITINERARIES OF SOME LEADING BUREAUCRATS*

BYATT, SIR HORACE.

British Central Africa, 1899–1904.
Somaliland, 1905–14.
Malta, 1914–16.
Tanganyika, 1916–24.
Trinidad, and Tobago (Governor), 1924–29.

CAMERON, SIR DONALD CHARLES.

British Guiana, 1890–1904.
Mauritius, 1904–7.
Nigeria, 1908–24 (Chief Secretary, 1921–24).
Tanganyika (Governor), 1924–31.
Nigeria (Governor), 1931–35.

DUNDAS, SIR CHARLES.

British East Africa, 1908–16.
Tanganyika, 1916–28.
Bahamas, 1928–34.
Northern Rhodesia, 1934–37.
Bahamas (Governor), 1937–40.
Uganda (Governor), 1940–44.

HARRISON, ERNEST.

South Africa (agricultural educator), 1910–17.
Kenya (Deputy Director of Agriculture), 1921–30.
Tanganyika, 1930–37.
Imperial College of Tropical Agriculture, Trinidad, 1938–43.

HOLLIS, SIR ALFRED CLAUD.

German East Africa (commercial representative), 1893–96.
British East Africa (Kenya), 1897–1912.
Sierra Leone, 1912–16.
Tanganyika, 1916–24.
Zanzibar (Resident), 1924–30.
Trinidad, and Tobago (Governor), 1930–35.

MACMICHAEL, SIR HAROLD.

Sudan, 1905–33.
Tanganyika, 1933–37.
Palestine (High Commissioner), 1938–44.

---

*These profiles are based on information contained in the footnotes of Ralph Austen's "The Official Mind of Indirect Rule: British Policy in Tanganyika, 1916–1939," in *Britain and Germany in Africa,* Prosser Gifford and Wm. Roger Louis, eds. (New Haven, 1967), pp. 577–606.

MITCHELL, SIR PHILIP EUEN.

Nyasaland, 1912–15.
East Africa campaign, 1915–18.
Nyasaland, 1918–19.
Tanganyika, 1919–35.
Uganda (Governor), 1935–40.
Middle East and East Africa Command, 1941–42.
Fiji and Western Pacific (Governor and High Commissioner), 1942–44.
Kenya (Governor), 1945–52.

SCOTT, SIR JOHN.

Ceylon, 1901–21.
Nigeria, 1921–24.
Tanganyika, 1924–29.
Straits Settlements (Governor), 1929–33.

SYMES, SIR STEWART.

Sudan (Army), 1900–20.
Palestine, 1920–28.
Aden (Resident), 1928–31.
Tanganyika, 1931–33.
Sudan (Governor), 1934–40.

WAKEFIELD, ARTHUR JOHN.

Northern Rhodesia, 1923–32.
Tanganyika, 1933–40.
West Indies, 1940–45.
East African Groundnuts Commission and Overseas Food Corporation, 1946–49.
Haiti and Peru (UN Technical Assistance), 1950–56.

NOTES

1. INTRODUCING THE BUREAUCRATIC ECONOMY: THE ABCs OF ORGANIZATION

1. *A Memorandum on the Economics of the Cattle Industry in Tanganyika by the Department of Veterinary Science and Animal Husbandry*, Sessional Paper no. 1, 1934 (Dar es Salaam, 1934), p. 12. A more complete listing of how some administrators perceived Tanganyika's ethnic groups and their "indigenous economic activities" can be found in *The Tribes of Tanganyika Territory, Their Districts, Usual Dietary and Pursuits* (Dar es Salaam, 1936), assembled primarily by R. C. Jerrard, then an assistant district officer in charge of labour. Public Record Office, London, Colonial Office file (henceforth CO) 691/152/42191/6. While much valuable information on local meteorological conditions and specific items of diet appears in that document, the fundamental categories of perception for "indigenous economic activity"—agricultural and/or pastoral—remain largely unrefined.

2. My favorite outsider's analysis of that ethos remains Robert Heussler's *Yesterday's Rulers* (Syracuse, 1963).

3. British Mandate for East Africa, *Supplement to the American Journal of International Law* 18 (July 1923):155.

4. CO 691/89. Minutes of June 24, 1927, meeting of the Permanent Mandates Commission.

5. The administration maintained that unofficial members were "nominated without regard to representation of particular races, interests, or public bodies," as suggested by the East Africa Commission Report of 1925. Selection of the first Legislative Council's unofficial roster in the mid-1920s brought protests from sections of the community which claimed either under-representation, such as the many Indian associations, or no representation at all, such as European residents of the Southern Highlands. M. P. Chitale, the Secretary of the Tanga Indian Association, asserted that both Indian unofficial members came from Dar es Salaam: one was a lawyer; the other, a wholesale trader. These backgrounds, he argued, did not reflect the variety of Indian interests in the territory. "We are not merely traders but are also planters and the trading communities of Tanganyika have different and distinct interests in three areas viz., in Tanga and hinterland mainly sisal, Mwanza and surrounding districts trading in native produce and interested in cotton cultivation and cotton ginning; Dar es Salaam mainly interested in wholesale trading." Tanzania National Archives Secretariat file (henceforth TNAS) 7339/1. M. P. Chitale to the Chief Secretary, October 1, 1926. The Chief Secretary responded on October 16, 1926, that the ". . . whole argument of the Association is based on the principle of representation whereas, as already explained, there is no representation as such on the Council." TNAS 7339/1/102.

6. Two agencies in Whitehall technically oversaw this relationship: the Colonial Office and the Treasury. The Colonial Office, in the persons of the Secretary of State for Colonies and the men on the Tanganyika desk, followed developments in the territory. The Secretary, responsible for defending colonial policy in Parliament, corresponded with the Tanganyika Governors on outstanding issues and required prior approval for some decisions, such as large land alienations. And he could reverse decisions already made—the power of disallowance. These were all prestigious monitors, but at this time their role was far more advisory than determinative. The Secretary never exercised the power of disallowance and the Tanganyika desk, which at times criticized the local administration's actions with considerable cogency, had a marginal impact on policy evolution. The Treasury inspected Tanganyika's annual budget and scrutinized requests for grants and loans. While this agency did not directly make policy for Tanganyika, it did intensify local revenue-consciousness by imposing rigorous borrowing criteria, which rested on the hallowed imperial principle that each territory should pay its own way as much as possible.

7. The Governor in conjunction with the Executive Council technically represented ultimate authority within the territory. But this council, which consisted of the Governor, chief secretaries, and department heads, never contradicted the chief executive. In fact, the council automatically endorsed the Governor's decisions and so invested them with a conciliar prestige. Secretary of Native Affairs Philip E. Mitchell captured the essence of this operation in his diary. Referring to an Executive Council meeting on December 31, 1930, he wrote, "It really is a farce, for D. C. [Donald Cameron] merely tells us what he proposes to do and then does it." Rhodes House Library, MSS. Afr. r. 101, Diaries of P. E. Mitchell, December 31, 1930. By permission of the Library.

8. One specialized department did devise a set of administrative categories with a better economic fit than provincial and district divisions. The Agriculture Department grouped those provinces and districts in four partial circles, covering the northeast, northwest, southeast, and southwest sections of the territory. These arcs represented more accurately the distribution of resources and sustained economic activity.

2. SERVICING THE BUREAUCRATIC ECONOMY: THE ABCs OF EXTRACTION

1. Rhodes House Library, MSS. Afr. r. 101, Diaries of P. E. Mitchell, July 15, 1930. By permission of the Library.

2. TNAS 13904. P. E. Mitchell minute, April 11, 1932. Some specialized departments did include in their annual published reports figures which show per capita departmental outlays on a racial basis but only in territorial aggregates. Still one can easily see why Mitchell was so forceful. Education and medical departments, for instance, disbursed their never generous allotments from the central administration in ways that made Africans bear a disproportionate burden of parsimony. Designating the contributions to particular tax yields by race would further specify who bore the onus of colonial administration.

3. *Annual Reports of the Provincial Commissioners on Native Administration for the Year 1934* (Dar es Salaam, 1935), p. 32.

4. *Annual Reports of the Provincial Commissioners on Native Administration for the Year 1938* (Dar es Salaam, 1939), p. 13.

5. *Annual Reports of the Provincial Commissioners on Native Administration for the Year 1937* (Dar es Salaam, 1938), p. 66.

6. TNAS 24852, I. Government Circular No. 33 of 1937 (December 2, 1937) also ordered that from January 1, 1938, labor contracts should specify "particulars" about "natives" (paragraph 4) and that workers not on contract should take out a road pass (*cheti cha njia*) detailing such facts (paragraph 5).

7. Tanzania National Archives (henceforth TNA) 967.822. A. W. M. Griffith, Tanga district report for 1932, no page numbers.

8. TNA 967.822. R. E. Seymour and E. C. Baker, Tanga district report for 1933, pp. 11–12.

9. Ibid., p. 13. Provincial Commissioner H. Hignell, Central, believed that "the amount of labour exacted in lieu of tax had to be nicely calculated as, otherwise, natives who could pay their tax would prefer to liquidate their debt to the Government by easy labour." That labor on "public works" was often not easy, but its calculation in tax-equivalents was always delicate, because some Africans at times acted as if working off their tax directly for Government involved fewer personal costs than obtaining the necessary coin from selling crops, wage-labor, trade, or other types of endeavor. Officers in the Central Province attempted to diminish the attractiveness which this mode of tax payment may have held for some by increasing the number of days "to be worked for a tax ticket," although as a consequence "we have not been able to employ as many tax defaulters during 1933 as during 1932." TNA 967.825. H. Hignell, Central Province Report for 1933, pp. 2–3.

10. TNA 967.822. E. C. Baker, Tanga district report for 1934, p. 29. A kipande is the card on which an employer marked completion of a worker's daily task; it should reveal at a glance how much more work a man had to put in to complete his contract.

11. CO 691/138/25157. G. Seel minute, August 9, 1934.

12. CO 691/153/42003. Note of interview with Major Scupham on November 18, 1937, regarding changes in "native" taxation.

13. CO 691/158/42224. Extracts from Pim Report (1937) on Financial Position and System of Taxation in Kenya with Marginal Comments by the Governor of Tanganyika (Harold A. MacMichael). The Governor, however, disputed the heavy incidence of taxation and, in an ironic acknowledgment of taxpayers as individuals, cited misleading per capita figures to support his point: "In Tanganyika Territory net tax proceeds therefore amount to about Shs. 2/– per head of the total African population."

14. TNAS 26298/II. S. McKnight to Chief Secretary, October 4, 1939. Chief Secretary to McKnight, November 2, 1939.

15. Communal taxation, never implemented during the inter-war period, was proposed to fit what some bureaucrats perceived as changing local group patterns. The term "commune" staked the fulcrum of taxation not on the district nor on the particular local society, but on the vague notion of community.

16. The author derived those numbers from an extensive survey of Native Treasury budgets, which appeared as appendices to the annual reports of the Provincial Commissioners. The primary "benefit" which the bureaucracy conferred upon "native" residents was a burgeoning local administrative structure. The real figures are probably higher, but they remain elusive. In Native Treasury categories other than "administrative expenses," such as education and health, the fraction of the budget devoted to local staff is not known. D. M. P. McCarthy, "The Economic Implications of Indirect Rule in Tanganyika, 1925–39" (unpublished seminar paper, Yale University, 1968), p. 17.

17. The interested reader should consult E. A. Brett's *Colonialism and Underdevelopment in East Africa* (New York, 1973), pp. 99–107, but remember that he sometimes falsely interchanges the concepts of customs union and common market.

18. The most salient example was the so-called sugar "consumption" tax, which began yielding revenue in 1933 (see table 2.2). Its rate was 3/– per 100 lbs on all sugar, other than that produced in Tanganyika. The Attorney General unavailingly argued that this levy was both mislabelled and offensive to the spirit of the Customs Agreements, because its real objective was to tax sugar entering Tanganyika from Kenya and Uganda. It did that, but the preference effectively accorded sugar produced in Kenya or Uganda and coming into Tanganyika was still 9/– per 100 lbs. For sugar imported directly from overseas confronted a real tariff wall of 12/– per 100 lbs, consisting of 6/– basic duty, 3/– "suspended duty," and 3/– "consumption" tax. Governor Symes had gone along with a Governors' Conference decision to reduce the "suspended duty" from 6/– to 3/– in 1933, but he won approval for the "consumption" tax, which maintained the height of the overseas tariff wall and, at the same time, fastened an extractive device on intra-regional trade. CO 691/126/31271. The "consumption" tax was expected to yield the Tanganyika administration about 10,000 pounds in revenue annually, and after a sub-par first year, it performed beyond that level.

19. Brett, for example, erroneously states that the principle of "suspended duties" allowed "individual territories to reduce the duty on most items by 10%" (p. 101).

20. TNAS 26939. Secretary G. K. Whitlamsmith, "Material for an Enquiry into the Effect on the Territory's Economy of the 'Suspended Duties' imposed on certain articles under the Authority of the Customs Tariff Ordinance, 1930, as amended," Central Development Committee Memorandum No. 32, CONFIDENTIAL, May 25, 1939. This entire memorandum is valuable, because it contains an exceptionally lucid contemporary analysis of the evolution of complementary and divergent economic and financial interests among the three East African territories during the inter-war period.

21. Wakefield recalled that in 1934 Government had to purchase disease-resistant wheat seed for free issue to indigent European farmers in Arusha. His views on "suspended duties" appear as an appendix to Whitlamsmith's memorandum.

22. The Tanganyika administration's reaction to Armitage-Smith's recommendations can be found in TNAS 13904.

23. TNAS 12564/I. Extract from an enclosure to Director of Agriculture's letter of February 23, 1933.

24. TNAS 21796. The petition itself was dated from Ujiji, August 28, 1933. P. E. Mitchell's minute, October 7, 1933. E. R. E. Surridge, Acting Chief Secretary, to Provincial Commissioner G. F. Webster, December 27, 1933. Its petition apparently brought the society increased administrative scrutiny. V. F. Wood, in a letter covering submission of the petition and written for the Provincial Commissioner to the Chief Secretary, concluded, on the basis of the district officer's information, that the Lake National is a "trading society whose members are numerous and composed entirely of the members of the Tanganyika Associations . . . that at present it exists almost solely by the individual efforts of the three signatories to the petition, Suleman Maftah, Kombo Baraka and Akilimali Mkweta, who, apparently, buy or take over on credit, the produce of the members and re-sell it." Wood suggested that "without skilled supervision, which cannot be given to the Lake National, such a venture is likely to end in failure, and loss to the members. It should be watched and not allowed to get too far into trouble." V. F. Wood for Provincial Commissioner to Chief Secretary, September 4, 1933.

25. While some members of the Tanganyika administration underscored the shackling effects of high freight rates, other policies reinforced the already favored position of rail transport. The bureaucracy, for instance, tried to prevent motor vehicles from competing too much with the railroad. Various restrictions, including vehicle licensing fees, and maintenance of a road "network" that fed rail lines instead of providing alternative routes all constrained the emergence of motor transport as a complete transportation mode.

26. TNAS 11871. P. E. Mitchell, February 6, 1933. Secretary of Economic Advisory Board to Chief Secretary, March 23, 1933, quoting extract from minutes of Economic Advisory Board meeting, March 20, 1933. G. J. Partridge minute, March 28, 1933. S. B. B. McElderry minute, March 28, 1933.

3. DEFINING TRADE AND TRADERS:
THE ENTRENCHMENT OF ECONOMIC INEQUITY

1. TNAS 30272. Appendix 3: Trade Licenses in Tanganyika Territory.

2. TNA 1733/24. P. E. Mitchell, Tanga district for 1923, p. 9.

3. TNAS 7092. This committee had five members. The Attorney General, E. St. J. Jackson, was chairman. Other participants were A. H. G. Prentice, Acting Treasurer; G. F. Webster, Acting Senior Commissioner, Dar es Salaam; Lt. Col. I. W. Massie, nominated by the Chamber of Commerce; and S. N. Chose, proposed by the Indian Association. Prentice and Massie both died during the committee's tenure. The report was issued on December 15, 1926.

4. Ibid. Committee Report, p. 5.

5. TNA Acc. 215/File 184. Secretariat Circular No. 88 of 1925. "Memo on Trade and Markets" by Donald Cameron, December 12, 1925, paragraph 4.

6. The 20/- special "native" license was a revenue producer. CO 691/77. D. Cameron to L. Amery, June 5, 1925. CONFIDENTIAL.

7. TNAS 7092. Committee Report, p. 5.

8. Ibid. "Objects and Reasons," E. St. J. Jackson, Attorney General, December 2, 1926.

9. Trades Licensing Ordinance of 1927, first published in Tanganyika Territory *Gazette* No. 52, then as amended in *Gazette* of December 10, 1926, pp. 683–87.

10. TNAS 7092. Trades Licensing Ordinance of 1927, report of Acting Attorney General, April 19, 1927, concerning amendments to bill in Legislative Council.

11. Ibid. J. Scott to L. S. Amery, June 16, 1927: ". . . the Form recommended by the Select Committee was somewhat inquisitorial and was admittedly designed to go beyond the simple requirements of a fiscal measure. The Governor considered that an

elaborate form of the nature proposed would create unnecessary difficulties to the small and semi-literate shopkeeper . . .''

The simplified schedule had nine questions and asked for (1) the name of the applicant; (2) the name of the business; (3) its address; (4) whether the business was a branch of another business in Tanganyika; (5) whether the business included wholesale trading; (6) whether it included retail trading only; (7) whether the business included export or import from beyond Tanganyika; and (8) whether it included purchases from ''natives'' of the produce of Tanganyika for resale in the territory. If respondent answered questions 5, 6, 7, and 8 in the negative, the ninth question asked that he state the nature of the business. On the Select Committee's form the phrasing of these questions was more peremptory.

12. Their official titles were: No. 1 of 1927: An Ordinance to provide for the licensing of persons carrying on businesses; No. 2 of 1927: An Ordinance to provide for the licensing of itinerant traders; and No. 3 of 1927: An Ordinance to repeal the Profits Tax Ordinance.

13. TNAS 7092/1. Treasurer to Chief Secretary, January 14, 1927.

14. Ibid. Illegibly signed Secretariat minute, January 25, 1927.

15. Ibid. ''Objects and Reasons'' for Itinerant Traders Ordinance, E. J. Macquarrie, Acting Attorney General, February 23, 1927.

16. P. E. Mitchell penned a memorable example of this bias in his diary: ''. . . the shopkeeper now rules the world and such minor persons as producers and consumers can never expect reasonable protection against his uncontrolled rapacity. The right to live like a blood sucking tick, on the community, and never do an honest day's work is now firmly established for the shopkeeper as inalienable and I should be torn to pieces were I to have at it: but I will have at it, if any sort of opportunity offers.'' Rhodes House Library, MSS. Afr. r. 101. Diaries of P. E. Mitchell, August 25, 1930. By permission of the Library.

17. The Markets Ordinance of 1928, with few modifications, came from Nigerian law. CO 691/96.

18. *Proceedings of the Legislative Council* (Dar es Salaam, 1930), third session, 1928/29, December 17, 1928, 1:38.

19. Mitchell diaries, February 23, 1931.

20. *Proceedings of the Legislative Council* (Dar es Salaam, 1935), ninth session, October 30, 1934, p. 61.

21. The Itinerant Traders (Amendment) Ordinance, 1932, made license refusal a more potent weapon. Before 1932 only the Governor had such power. Under the revised legislation any local licensing authority could deny an application, subject to review by the appropriate Provincial Commissioner and then Governor. A 1936 amendment enveloped ''commercial travellers'' and so regulated ''any person . . . not being ordinarily resident in the Territory'' who ''solicits orders for goods on behalf of other persons but does not include a person employed as a traveller by a person licensed under the Trades Licensing Ordinance.''

22. The 1928 Markets bill had proved somewhat ineffective. At a Government House conference in December 1931, Director of Agriculture Harrison and Provincial Commissioner Hignell, Central, complained about the impact which the ''itinerant trader system'' had on official market organization. ''Practices [of these traders] were difficult to control and by transacting business on the borders of townships he [the itinerant trader] stifled the development of markets and trading centres.'' Effective control of itinerant trading required a longer radius, but the Governor was not prepared to repress such exchange completely. Harrison and Hignell argued that because itinerant trading lacked ''a variety of stock,'' it failed to ''stimulate trade.'' How small-scale mobile traders might carry this ''variety'' and still maintain a necessary floating inventory of such common goods as clothing articles and matches is not clear. The Governor did not rebut the Harrison-Hignell position directly, but proposed a different justification for itinerant traders. They transported ''native'' produce to collection points and, if removed, might not supply ''necessary transport facilities.'' This type of trading was, then, more crucial, from the Governor's viewpoint, on the supply than on the demand side. Contrasting supply and demand arguments produced a compromise at the 1931 conference: ''It was decided that steps

might be taken to exclude the itinerant trader from certain districts in which a proper marketing system could be established without his assistance." TNAS 20464. Notes on a Conference held at Government House, December 14, 1931.

23. "Media as Ends: Money and the Underdevelopment of Tanganyika to 1940," *The Journal of Economic History*, 36 (September 1976):645–62.

24. *Proceedings of the Legislative Council* (Dar es Salaam, 1933), sixth session, February 5, 1932, 1:91–94.

25. Ibid., p. 96.

26. Ibid., p. 97.

27. TNAS 20464. E. Harrison memorandum on "Marketing of Native Export Crops." He cited as precedents the Uganda Coffee and Nyasaland Tobacco Ordinances.

28. *Proceedings of the Legislative Council* (Dar es Salaam, 1933), sixth session, February 5, 1932, 1:95.

29. CO 691/123/31088. G. Seel minute, April 12, 1932.

30. Ibid. J. F. N. Green minute, February 24, 1932.

31. Ibid. Seel minute.

32. Ibid. P. Cunliffe-Lister minute, May 2, 1932.

33. Ibid. Green approved the Trades Licensing (Amendment) Ordinance with the narrow application of exclusive licenses, but observed that this proceeding was "another instance of the practice, so unfortunately common, of passing legislation which goes far beyond the object aimed at. Governors are always apologizing for bad laws by saying that they are carefully administered." July 8, 1932, minute.

34. By 1935 only two had been issued: one for cashew nuts in the Eastern Province; a second for beeswax in the Morogoro district. TNAS 20614. G. F. Sayers, Acting Chief Secretary, to Honorary Secretary, Federated Chamber of Commerce Section, the Indian Association, May 17, 1935. The beeswax case demonstrates the restraining power of the Indian Association. Acting Director of Agriculture Wakefield wrote in 1936 that Mr. B. Merali wished to surrender his license: "It is known that his reason for this is the pressure which has been brought to bear on him by the Indian Association." Wakefield reported that Merali had informed the District Officer, Morogoro, "that he had been privately warned that it would be better for him to give it up." And "it appears that the warning was no idle one." Then Wakefield asserted, "No Indian firm of repute would apply" for such an exclusive license, and only one European firm might be interested. TNAS 20614. A. J. Wakefield to Chief Secretary, May 9, 1936. CONFIDENTIAL. The Merali case becomes clouded after September 1936. He changed his mind and wished to retain the license, but on March 4, 1939, the only exclusive license in force was for Eastern Province cashew nuts, held by Messrs. Gibson and Company. TNAS 26600. Trades Licensing Ordinance, Overhaul of Part II. I do not know what happened to Merali, but the Indian Association evidently succeeded in its lobbying.

35. TNAS 30272. Committee membership: the Treasurer, Provincial Commissioner (Dar), Mr. Adamjee, Mr. Massie, Dr. Malik, and Mr. Stewart. An Indian presence guaranteed that revisions proposed by the Indian Association would be heard, though not necessarily heeded.

36. TNAS 22872. Report of the Committee to Enquire into the Trades Licensing Ordinance of 1927, Dar es Salaam, October 24, 1935, p. 4.

37. Ibid. Committee Report, p. 14 (schedule of definitions).

38. Ibid. Committee Report, pp. 5, 13.

39. Ibid. Minute of Attorney General, February 18, 1936.

40. Among the exempted businesses were those of a planter, farmer, stock raiser, market gardener, or dairyman, who dealt only in the produce of his own estate.

41. TNAS 22872. Acting Provincial Commissioner, Lake, to Chief Secretary, January 6, 1936.

42. TNAS 30272. Official commentary on 1935 Trades Licensing Committee Report.

43. TNA 967.825. A. V. Hartnoll, Dodoma district for 1927, pp. 13–14.

44. TNAS 23850. Memo on Trades Licensing Draft Bill by Executive Committee of the Federated Chamber of Commerce Section of the Indian Association, Dar es Salaam, October 6, 1936, pp. 4–5.

45. And consider the prosecutorial possibilities of this interpretation of an itinerant trader. Treasurer R. W. Taylor circularized in 1930 that "once a consumer or producer comes to him, he ceases to be itinerant and needs a licence under Section 6(1)(d) of T. L. O." TNA Acc. 215/184. Trades Licensing Commissioners' Circular Instruction No. 3. Treasury, January 2, 1930. Who seeks out whom in mobile trading is often arguable and so there is much room for conclusions adverse to itinerant traders.

46. TNAS 23850. D. M. Kennedy's marginal note on the Indian Association's memorandum.

47. It is impossible to quantify the distribution of different types of traders over time from official reports, but there are extensive district-by-district figures showing the kinds of licenses issued for 1935 in TNAS 24324.

48. TNAS 23850. Recommendations section of Indian Association memorandum.

49. Ibid. G. R. Sandford minute on Indian Association memorandum, October 21, 1936.

50. Relations between certain licenses and the restrained consumption of particular commodities also received some attention. The official 1935 Trades Licensing Enquiry committee recommended partial deregulation of butchers' activities. "Natives should be encouraged to eat meat," the Committee asserted, "and butchers' licenses may tend to operate in restraint of its consumption. Many natives would purchase and slaughter an occasional ox on favourable occasions for sale as meat but are at present deterred by the necessity of paying a Shs. 20/- fee." The Committee recommended specific butchers' licenses only for shops located in a township or minor settlement. R. R. Scott, Director of Medical Services, objected, because this change "would encourage shops on outskirts of townships, where meat is not liable to inspection nor control"; tapeworm disease was so serious a problem that no relaxation was possible. According to Provincial Commissioner F. J. Bagshawe, Western, this movement was already happening around Tabora but in response to different rules and taxes. To avoid compulsory slaughter at abattoirs with inspection and fees, over thirty "native butchers" had left the town and started business within a few yards of the boundary, where they sold to Tabora's inhabitants (including Europeans) about 90 percent of the meat consumed: ". . . though I have heard of no unfortunate results, I see enough of these transboundary meat stalls to consume from the 10%." In any event, administrators rejected deregulation for medical and revenue reasons. TNAS 22872. Committee Report, p. 12. R. R. Scott to Chief Secretary, December 12, 1935. F. J. Bagshawe to Chief Secretary, January 3, 1936.

The bureaucracy did concede that licensing fees restrained the distribution and consumption of dried fish. The Nutrition Committee had recommended that to cheapen its price and "make it more readily available," its sellers should be exempted from the Itinerant Traders Ordinance. Fresh produce was already excluded, but not dried fish: "We are satisfied that the present license fee acts as a deterrent to the distribution of this commodity." TNAS 20621. Extract from Nutrition Committee Report. The revised 1938 Itinerant Traders Ordinance so exempted.

4. RESTRICTING AFRICAN ACCESS TO CREDIT:
THE ENLARGEMENT OF DEPENDENT OPPORTUNITY

1. Rhodes House Library, MSS. Afr. s. 1072. Reports and memoranda, Tanganyika, by Frank Collings Hallier. Rufiji district report, April 10, 1920, p. 3. By permission of the Library and the family.

2. Hallier, p. 5.

3. British Mandate for East Africa, *Supplement to the American Journal of International Law* 18 (July 1923):155.

4. Tanganyika Territory *Gazette*, 1923.

5. *Bouvier's Law Dictionary* (Baldwin's Century Edition), W. E. Baldwin, ed., p. 254. This standard lexicon enumerates three additional meanings of credit:

1. That which is due to a merchant, as distinguished from debit, that which is due by him;

2. That influence connected with certain social positions (20 Toullier, no. 19);

3. In a statute making credits the subject of taxation, the term is held to mean the excess of the sum of all legal claims and demands, whether for money or other valuable thing, or for labor or services, due or to become due to the person liable to pay taxes thereon, when added together (estimating every such claim or demand at its true value in money) over and above the sum of all legal *bona fide* debts owing by such person (37 Ohio St. 123).

6. TNA 1733/24. P. E. Mitchell, Tanga district report for 1923, p. 1.

7. TNAS 18858. P. E. Mitchell minute, February 3, 1931.

8. TNAS 13698. Donald Cameron minute, December 5, 1930.

9. *Proceedings of the Legislative Council* (Dar es Salaam, 1931), fourth session, 1929/30, February 11, 1930, p. 156.

10. Ibid., February 12, 1930, p. 177.

11. Ibid., p. 172.

12. TNAS 10493. Extract from an address presented to H. E. the Governor by Indian Community of Tabora, April 26, 1930.

13. TNAS 18858. Cutting from *Tanganyika Standard,* October 27, 1930.

14. In 1937 the administration added another amendment, which placed the "native holder" of a coffee dealer's license issued under the Coffee Industry (Registration and Improvement) Ordinance, 1936, in the same position as a "native holder" of a license issued under the Trades Licensing and Itinerant Traders Ordinances. Coffee dealers were thus exempted from the debt irrecoverability provisions of Section 3 of the Credit to Natives (Restriction) Ordinance, 1931. TNAS 10493.

15. TNAS 10493. Memorandum regarding the alterations in the law introduced by the Credit to Natives (Restriction) Ordinance, 1931. D. J. Jardine, Chief Secretary.

16. CO 691/119/30184. Legal report by Attorney General on amended ordinance to restrict credit to "natives."

17. *Proceedings of the Legislative Council* (Dar es Salaam, 1932), fifth session, May 5, 1931, 2:17.

18. TNAS 26231. Donald Cameron minute, June 18, 1929.

19. TNAS 10493. Conference of Governors of British East African Territories, February 1933. Note by Governor of Tanganyika on "Native Policy: Credit Sales to Natives" (Dar es Salaam, February 19, 1933), paragraph 4.

20. Ibid., paragraph 2.

21. *Proceedings of the Legislative Council* (Dar es Salaam, 1931), fourth session, 1929/30, February 12, 1930, p. 179.

22. TNAS 10493. Secretariat Circular No. 29 of 1932, D. J. Jardine, Chief Secretary.

23. Ibid. Note on "Native Policy: Credit Sales to Natives," paragraph 3.

24. Ibid. Report of Symes's remarks in extract from proceedings of Governors' Conference, February 1933.

25. Ibid. Note on "Native Policy: Credit Sales to Natives," paragraph 2.

26. Administrators correctly decided that during the inter-war period mortgaging rather than selling land was the more important problem. But in some areas, particularly the larger population centers, a land market had emerged, despite legal prohibitions. The situation around Dar es Salaam was most disturbing. In his 1939 paper on the "Extent and Conditions under which Natives are occupying land in the outskirts of Dar es Salaam," H. H. McCleery observed and analyzed that process. Although no freehold title could in theory be purchased from government, "non-natives can and do acquire freehold land by purchase from the natives [p. 9]." He feared the consequences of a belt of land around the city permanently alienated to non-Africans: "Rents for agricultural land will rise, and with it the price of native food. The natives' cost of living will rise, and we shall be faced with the evils of speculation, rack-renting, and a landless peasantry."

Also irritating was a fact which diverged from bureaucratic visions of a stolid, homogeneous African peasantry: "A number of wealthy natives employ labourers to cultivate for them on Crown land." Though reluctant to discourage "private enterprise," McCleery urged that this practice be stopped: "A native should only be allowed as much land as he and his family can cultivate [p. 7]." Should land law accommodate and perhaps regulate changing market conditions? No. The administration should never legally grant freehold tenure to Africans; this would accelerate the "growth of a landless peasantry, since the improvident will dispose of their land." And "quite apart from the serious disorders that will result from the growth of a landless class, there is the moral aspect. We are, after all, Trustees for the natives, and so long as this Territory is a Mandate we must safeguard their land [p. 18]."

The "safeguards" did not win an enthusiastic reception. Few "natives" requested a right of occupancy, the principal administrative artifice confirming legal possession of land. At the 31st session of the Permanent Mandates Commission, June 2, 1937, Lord Hailey asked Mr. Nicoll, the Tanganyikan representative, "Was it a fact that applications had not been made by natives for rights of occupancy except in urban areas?" Nicoll said, "So far, yes." CO 691/153/42009. Minutes of the 31st session of the Permanent Mandates Commission, fourth meeting, June 2, 1937. Not until 1937 did the administration introduce the "safeguard" of a written agreement between Africans occupying land and "non-natives" about to displace them in cases of alienation. From that time local officers were to consider the capacity of the Africans' new plot for absorbing the expansion of the affected "native" family. CO 691/160.

27. TNAS 18823. R. W. Taylor, Treasurer, to Chief Secretary, March 13, 1930.

28. TNAS 21920. Acting Treasurer to Chief Secretary, June 9, 1933.

29. Ibid. P. E. Mitchell minute, July 25, 1933.

30. Ibid. D. J. Jardine minute, July 29, 1933.

31. Ibid. Treasury, Circular Instruction No. 9, August 24, 1933.

32. Ibid. L. S. Guerning to Chairman, House Tax Commissioners, Dar es Salaam, September 14, 1933.

33. Ibid. P. E. Mitchell minute, November 25, 1933.

34. Ibid.

35. In 1936 the administration revised the "native" tax ordinance and reversed nomenclature. The amended Native House and Poll Tax Ordinance contained perhaps as elastic a definition of house as was the original description of hut. This change ended some administrative arguments over houses v. huts and may have removed those disincentives to dwelling improvement. But the switch comes too close to the end of the inter-war period for me to tell. However, I doubt that changing the fiscal designation of African dwellings from huts to houses significantly upgraded their acceptability as collateral. And jumping from one embracing stereotype to another stretched house too far. To call a real hovel a house undermined language as much as naming some substantial African houses huts.

36. TNAS 10493. This file contains an extract from a petition by the President, Bukoba African Association, presented during the Governor's tour in 1934, and Mac-Michael's notes on his "interview" with the Association.

37. Ibid. Issa bin Imangi to H. E., September 15, 1932. I do not know whether the Governor ever saw this letter.

38. Ibid. Chief Secretary to Provincial Commissioner, Lake, September 23, 1932.

39. TNAS 18858. D. J. Jardine minute, May 7, 1930.

5. ORGANIZING OFFICIAL MARKETS: WINNERS AND LOSERS

1. *Proceedings of the Legislative Council* (Dar es Salaam, 1930), third session, 1928/29, 1:41.

2. *Proceedings of the Legislative Council* (Dar es Salaam, 1934), eighth session, 1933/34, November 7, 1933, p. 65. When the Indian Association called in the mid-1930s for a radical reorganization of the market system, the administration demurred and con-

tinued to insist that "the main objects" of the present arrangement "are to ensure that the grower should obtain cash for his produce and a fair market price, having regard to world prices and locality and production." TNAS 20614. G. J. Partridge, for Acting Chief Secretary, to Secretary, Federated Chamber of Commerce Section, the Indian Association, May 17, 1935.

3. CO 691/73. Seventh report of cotton specialist Wood, October 21, 1924.

4. TNAS 20464. E. Harrison memorandum on "Marketing of Native Export Crops" presented to Conference held at Government House, Dar es Salaam, December 14, 1931, p. 2.

5. Ibid., p. 6.

6. CO 691/78. Gloss on 1924 Administrators' Conference, Dar es Salaam.

7. For the "right" to sell goods within a center the seller paid to lessee, depending on the particular local arrangement, a stall rental fee or, if one chose not to rent, tolls on products sold in that market. Some markets had byelaws that imposed paper limits on those charges. The Tabora market byelaws, for instance, permitted a lessee to collect rental fees on meat sellers, liquor vendors, and auctioneers of up to 1/- per diem, on fish sellers of up to -/50 (fifty cents), and on vendors of fruit, vegetables, firewood, and charcoal of up to -/20 (twenty cents). Some legally certified Township Markets were managed directly by their local Township Authorities, but this setup only changed the destination of transactions charges. In the Moshi Township Market, for example, each meat stall-holder paid fifty cents per diem to the Township Authorities; those who sold poultry and other feathered game returned six cents; other stall-holders paid "6% of the sum realised by the sale of their produce provided that if the amount realised be less than Sh. 1/- the fee shall be 3 cents and if less than 50 cents no fee shall be charged." Both Tabora and Moshi fee schedules come from byelaws implemented in the early 1930s and preserved in TNAS 12036.

8. TNAS 23283. Minute by R. H. Drayton, Attorney General, on amendments to Markets legislation, February 5, 1936.

9. Ibid. H. A. MacMichael minute, February 11, 1936.

10. Ibid. H. Hignell to A. Sillery, personal letter, February 19, 1936.

11. TNAS 20776, III. Mwanza Market Bye-Laws for 1933. D. C. Campbell minute, June 30, 1933. G. J. Partridge minute, July 1, 1933.

12. TNAS 12036. Kahama Market Bye-Laws for 1931. This file contains other market byelaws which are not cited.

13. TNAS 11871. P. E. Mitchell minute, February 6, 1933.

14. TNA 1733/6/60. Malangali district report for 1925, p. 2.

15. TNA 967.823. Kondoa-Irangi district report for 1933, p. 12.

16. TNA File 1548. Lake Province report which contains 1938 district report, p. 4.

17. TNAS 20776/II. Provincial Commissioner C. Richards, Lake, to Chief Secretary, March 28, 1933.

18. TNAS 12036. Minute by A. E. Kitching, Acting Chief Secretary, April 21, 1931.

19. TNA 1733/4/52. Tabora district report for 1925, p. 7.

20. TNA 1733/20/105. Shinyanga sub-district report for 1925, pp. 5-6.

21. TNA 967.823. W. S. G. Barnes, Kondoa-Irangi district report for 1929, pp. 12-13.

22. TNA 1733/4/52. Tabora district report for 1925, p. 7.

23. Governor Cameron had urged in this circular that ". . . the native should be free to sell his produce without the intervention of the State, like any producer" and "if natives ask for a market where they can sell their produce in the belief that they will get better prices there, everything should be done to meet their wishes." TNA Acc. 215/File 184. Secretariat Circular No. 88 of 1925, Cameron memorandum on Trade and Markets, December 12, 1925.

24. This decision provoked strong opposition, as the Indian community at Dodoma protested the granting of licenses to persons outside recognized trade centers. Government responded that it could not create a trading monopoly for townships and trading centers only. TNA 967.825. Acting Provincial Commissioner Longland, Central Province report for 1926, p. 20.

25. TNA 967.825. A. V. Hartnoll, Dodoma district report for 1926 (old Dodoma sub-district), pp. ix–x.
26. TNA 967.825. A. V. Hartnoll, Dodoma district report for 1927, p. 15.
27. Ibid., p. 16.
28. TNA 30/6/1927. H. Hignell, Half-year report for Central Province, pp. 16–17, which also contains Governor's commentary.
29. Ibid., p. 18.
30. TNA 967.825. C. B. Wilkins, Dodoma district report for 1928, p. 2.
31. Ibid., pp. 16–17.
32. Ibid., pp. 17–18.
33. Ibid., p. 19.
34. TNA 967.825. H. Hignell, Central Province report for 1932, p. 2.
35. TNAS 11871. Provincial Commissioner C. Richards, Lake, to Chief Secretary, June 27, 1932.
36. Ibid. Chief Secretary to Richards, August 3, 1932.
37. TNA PC 1/17. Musoma district report for 1925, pp. 1–2.
38. TNA 77/A. A. W. M. Griffith, Bukoba district report for 1926, pp. 23–24. Inter-mixing economic with ethical judgments sometimes produced intriguing results. Officer Hatchel, writing on Mwanza district for 1927, criticized Indian traders for lacking commercial "morality," but then added that "driven by the devil competitive prices the Indian merchant cuts his retail prices to the lowest possible figure." TNA PC 1/30. Mwanza district report for 1927, p. 18. (Would that more final consumers had benefited from practices that reduced prices to the "lowest possible figure.") Hatchel may have had in mind a two-tier distinction in profit levels which Officer Jones made explicit in the 1928 Mwanza report. Jones noted that Indian traders, who handled most retail sales in that district, usually had little capital; they got their goods on a ninety-day credit basis; and their main objective was "to realise as quickly as possible so that the cash thus available can be employed before settling day on the purchase of produce from the native." The actual "profit," Jones suggested, on the sale of trade goods was small, but the cash so obtained was used to buy produce which was then sold at a moderate profit. There were, then, at least two different profit levels in this case: a small one from retailing; and a larger but not excessive one from reselling African produce. TNA PC 1/53. S. B. Jones, for district officer (absent on duty), Mwanza district report for 1928, p. 16.
39. TNA Acc. 215/File 184. F. W. Brett to Chief Secretary, August 28, 1925.
40. TNA Lake Province 1136. J. L. Fairclough, Bukoba district report for 1937, pp. 10–11.
41. TNA 967.823. W. S. G. Barnes, Kondoa-Irangi district report for 1929, p. 13.

6. MANIPULATING AGRICULTURE: THE "PLANT-MORE-CROPS" CAMPAIGN

1. TNA 967.825. H. Hignell, Half-yearly report on the Central Province, June 30, 1928, p. 1.
2. *Proceedings of the Legislative Council* (Dar es Salaam, 1933), sixth session, January 26, 1932, 1:4.
3. TNAS 18687. R. W. Taylor to Chief Secretary, January 24, 1930.
4. Rhodes House Library, MSS. Afr. r. 101, Diaries of P. E. Mitchell, November 26, 1932. By permission of the Library.
5. TNA PC 1/53. W. F. Page, Kwimba district report for 1928, p. 9.
6. *Report of the Department of Agriculture for 1931* (Dar es Salaam, 1932), p. 44.
7. CO 691/157/42167. F. Lee minute, November 1937.
8. The area of government abstention was, according to A. J. Wakefield, an "isosceles triangle with its apex at Mombo and its base at Pangani and Tanga." TNAS 26298/I. Director of Agriculture Wakefield, points for letter to provincial commissioners, October 27, 1938.

9. Rhodes House Library, MSS. Afr. s. 900(1), Diaries of C. Gillman, XII, May 9, 1935. By permission of the Library and the family.

10. I analyze this incident in "Organizing Underdevelopment from the Inside: The Bureaucratic Economy in Tanganyika, 1919–1940," *The International Journal of African Historical Studies,* 10 (1977):597–98.

11. *Report of the Department of Agriculture for 1934* (Dar es Salaam, 1935), pp. 7–8.

12. *Report of the Department of Agriculture for 1935* (Dar es Salaam, 1936), p. 6.

13. Ibid., p. 9.

14. Please consult "Language Manipulation in Colonial Tanganyika, 1919–40," *Journal of African Studies,* 6 (Spring 1979):9–16.

15. CO 691/45. H. A. Byatt to Secretary of State for Colonies, June 16, 1921.

16. TNAS 26298/3, v. I. W. E. H. Scupham to Provincial Commissioner, Southern Highlands, concerning Secretariat general letter on campaign with specifics for each province, December 1938.

17. TNAS 26298/6, v. II. A. J. Wakefield, September 16, 1939. These crops should be encouraged "where supplies of groundnut seed are scarce."

18. TNAS 26298/I. A. J. Wakefield, Notes for Ginners' Meeting Held at Morogoro, November 12, 1938. These notes are redlined "Personal: not for publication in any form."

19. The author analyzes those guidelines in that aforementioned "Language Manipulation" article. Some local officers continued to invest "permissible pressure" with new meanings. D. A. G. Dallas, district officer for Rufiji, was perhaps the most imaginative. On January 7, 1939, he wrote Provincial Commissioner Longland, Eastern, that it was "necessary to stimulate production of more crops of every kind: (a) by persuasion and publicity in the first place and, if this method fails, (b) by compulsion." Dallas proposed a prize scheme which would reward the chiefs and headmen for the best cotton shamba and other achievements; the manager of the Liverpool Uganda Company had already promised to furnish the prizes. Longland objected to prizes for chiefs and headmen: "As I say Captain Dallas is full of zeal." The Secretariat agreed with Longland but left open the possibility of commercial fairs with prizes. Dallas then suggested, and received approval for, aerial inspections of his district. Director Wakefield reported to the Secretariat in April 1939 a flight which he and Dallas made over the Rufiji district on February 22: "The propaganda value of the aeroplane flying over the various areas has proved to be very great and natives everywhere are responding very well to the pressure of propaganda." After the flight, Wakefield noted, "suitable exhortations" were sent out to the headmen of the respective areas flown over. TNAS 26298/7, v. I. D. A. G. Dallas to F. Longland, January 7, 1939. F. Longland to Chief Secretary, January 17, 1939. A. L. Pennington, Secretariat minute, January 18, 1939. TNAS 26298/7, v. II. A. J. Wakefield to E. R. E. Surridge, Secretariat, April 6, 1939.

20. TNAS 26298/I. A. J. Wakefield to W. E. H. Scupham, November 12, 1938. CONFIDENTIAL.

21. Ibid. A. J. Wakefield, Notes for Ginners' Meeting, November 12, 1938.

22. Ibid. A. J. Wakefield, points for letter to provincial commissioners, October 27, 1938.

23. TNAS 26298/1. A. J. Wakefield to W. E. H. Scupham, October 1938.

24. TNAS 26298/2, v. II. O. G. Williams to District Commissioners Tabora and Nzega, October 25, 1940. CONFIDENTIAL.

25. TNAS 26298/4. A. J. Wakefield, September 21, 1939.

26. TNAS 26298/4. D. A. G. Dallas to Provincial Commissioner, Eastern, February 4, 1940.

27. TNAS 26298/1, v. II. F. C. Hallier to Chief Secretary, July 12, 1939.

28. *Report of the Department of Agriculture for 1938* (Dar es Salaam, 1939), p. 7.

29. Some Native Authorities ordered "every native" to plant sufficient foodstuffs, but British officers often wrote as if this phrase designated "every able-bodied male head of household." The meanings of household can vary from one society to another, but I am unequipped to assess what special problems enforcement created for the particular social operation of any given local society. The argument concerning food market retardation

should still apply in most cases, because autarky was imposed on what the British deemed physical production units—small farms or shambas—regardless of their social significance.
   30. CO 691/175/42303/39. G. L. M. Clauson minute, October 9, 1939. H. Tempany minute, December 11, 1939.

7. REGULATING THE COTTON INDUSTRY: THE FUTILITY OF PAPER PROTEST

   1. District Officer W. Ronayne, Rufiji, explained what many other local officials also confronted. "Cotton is a most unpopular crop," he noted, "and its extension has defied all efforts of the department of agriculture over a long period of years. Year after year, large quantities of free seed have been distributed, practical instruction has been given, vigorous propaganda has been employed, political pressure has been applied, prize-giving even has been resorted to; yet, the prejudice, deep-rooted as it must be against this crop remains unmoved. . . . This prejudice is occasioned by the belief that the monetary return for the amount of labour involved makes cotton-growing an uneconomic type of proposition." TNA Rufiji district report for 1931 (3/VI/D), p. 6.
   2. CO 691/63. A. H. Kirby, memo no. 123/2/2479 on proposals for a grant to agriculture funds from ECGC, August 27, 1923.
   3. Mr. Wood, a cotton specialist representing the ECGC in Tanganyika, had prepared detailed criticisms of government approaches but reflected the magnitude of his employer's general disillusionment when he called for "a clear statement of Policy, leaving the details for each District to be filled in by discussion between the Administrative and the Agricultural service. . . ." CO 691/72. Sixth report of cotton specialist Wood, July 9, 1924. All he got was the general Kirby line varnished for presentation to the Secretary of State for Colonies: ". . . the policy of this Government has been clear from the outset, namely to produce more and better cotton where it can be successfully grown without endangering the cultivation of native foodstuffs and in such localities where markets are available for disposal of the crop under safeguards which are contained in the Cotton Rules." CO 691/72. Acting Governor J. Scott to Secretary of State for Colonies, October 14, 1924.
   4. CO 691/72. J. Scott to Secretary of State for Colonies, September 16, 1924, telegram.
   5. TNAS 18681 and 10047/vol. Ia. Minutes of seventh meeting, January 9, 1930. This policy, Acting Director of Agriculture H. Wolfe wrote the Chief Secretary on January 18, requires "alteration of law relating to the sale by auction of the leases of ginnery sites and ginnery buying posts." The protection of existing ginneries from competition would not be complete "if outside interests are permitted to bid for the site in competition with that ginnery." Estimated new production might justify bids from others to a figure which an "existing ginnery would consider uneconomic." TNAS 18681. H. Wolfe to Chief Secretary, January 18, 1930.
   Governor Cameron supported the necessary change in the 1923 Land Ordinance on the grounds that here uneconomic competition might produce an excessive or "uneconomic rent" for sites, which would reduce prices to the "native producer who, in his turn, is a sufferer." TNAS 18681. D. Cameron to Secretary of State Passfield, March 5, 1930. The resulting 1930 amendment inserted in section 14 of that 1923 ordinance (chapter 68 of revised edition of Laws) "cotton ginneries" and "cotton buying posts" as more instances of the "certain purposes" for which Government could grant a right of occupancy without auctioning land.
   6. TNAS 10047/v. Ia. H. Wolfe to Chief Secretary, April 14, 1930.
   7. TNAS 18681. Memo by D. Cameron on principles to be followed in considering applications for sites for the purchase of cotton, enclosure No. 3 to dispatch of May 21, 1930. Preserving an "element of competition" does "not, of course, apply to areas where a ginnery has a restricted monopoly on a sliding scale agreement."
   8. TNAS 10047/v. IIa. Summary of Eastern Province Cotton Conference, December 8, 1932.

9. TNAS 10047/v. III. E. Harrison to Chief Secretary, January 20, 1933, covering letter for minutes of January 12 meeting of CAB.

10. TNAS 10047/v. IIa. Cotton Notes by the Director of Agriculture, February 19, 1934.

11. TNAS 10047/v. IIa. System of arriving at minimum price payable: take full price Liverpool middling four months futures in pence, subtract 10 percent from total to cover margin, then subtract 2.50 (buying and realisation charges); divide remainder by 18.2 for kilogram areas or by 40.0 for avoirdupois areas and the result is the cents/kilo or cents/pound of seed cotton delivered at ginnery.

12. Unless otherwise noted, all evidence cited in the section "Paper Protest in the Eastern Province" comes from TNAS 22895.

13. Saleh Yusuf Mkoma, Saleke Amari, et al., to Chief Secretary, February 28, 1935.

14. R. B. Richardson to Saleh Yusuf Mkoma, March 8, 1935.

15. African Planters Association to Chief Secretary, February 23, 1935.

16. Acting Chief Secretary to African Planters Association, March 12, 1935.

17. E. Harrison minute, March 11, 1935.

18. TNAS 10047/v. IIa. Harrison's Cotton Notes, February 19, 1934.

19. G. F. Webster minute, March 14, 1935.

20. Extract from *Tanganyika Opinion (Daily)*, March 23, 1935.

21. Extract from "Why Kill Free Trade?" in *Tanganyika Herald*, March 23, 1935.

22. Extract from *Tanganyika Herald*, March 29, 1935.

23. African Planters Association to Chief Secretary, March 26, 1935.

24. E. Harrison minute, March 1935, not dated.

25. Minute by Solicitor General, May 9, 1935.

26. Acting Chief Secretary to Salehe bin Yusufu, Kilosa, May 18, 1935.

27. D. C. Campbell minute, May 13, 1935.

28. Mr. Nicoll's minute.

29. G. F. Sayers minute, May 14, 1935.

30. "Note regarding Protest of A.P.A. of Morogoro against the restriction on the movement of unginned cotton from certain areas, and asking that existing cotton markets be continued," May 15, 1935.

31. Undated minute by unknown author.

32. H. A. MacMichael minute, September 3, 1935.

33. D. C. Campbell to Provincial Commissioner, Eastern, September 11, 1935.

34. The African Planters Association, Morogoro and Kilosa, to Chief Secretary, January 13, 1936.

35. D. C. Campbell to President, APA, January 23, 1936.

36. N. V. Rounce, Agricultural Officer, to Director of Agriculture, April 17, 1936, "A Record of the Requests of a Deputation of the Morogoro Native Cotton Planters Association."

37. E. E. Hutchins to A. J. Wakefield, April 24, 1936. CONFIDENTIAL.

38. Relating output changes only to numbers and kinds of buyers in any location was a precarious exercise. The authors of an inside document, prepared to rebut another APA complaint about the poor quality of available seed, presented some meteorological facts which must be considered. "There is no evidence," they concluded, "to show that the low yields obtained over the past three years [in areas of eastern Tanganyika] are due to the seed planted, unfavourable climatic factors are more likely to be the cause: rains practically failed in 1933, they were abnormally late and too heavy in 1934, and again this year carried on too long for cotton." Extract from a "Note for His Excellency on cotton seed supplies which matter will be brought to his notice by the Morogoro Planters." That note was more illuminating in its weather summary than in its rejoinder to the seed complaint. The APA wanted higher quality seed from whatever source as soon as possible. The Agriculture Department responded that in a selection of local plant types lies the "best means of improving yield and possible quality," that investigation of best strains was a "slow process," and that research on Barberton U/4 types was going on at experimental stations in the territory.

39. A. J. Wakefield to Chief Secretary, April 23, 1936. CONFIDENTIAL.

40. The Cotton Advisory Board's unofficial membership "has been changed from time to time to meet the agitations of both middlemen and those ginners who did not happen to be on the Board." TNAS 10047/v. III. A. J. Wakefield to W. E. H. Scupham, September 1, 1936. The original 1927 roster had as officials the Director of Agriculture (always the chairman), the Secretary of Native Affairs, and the Comptroller of Customs; unofficials were two people nominated by the Tanganyika Ginneries Association and one proposed by the Mwanza Chamber of Commerce. The Eastern Province Cotton Buyers Association protested in 1932 that the CAB "over-represented the ginners and under-represented cotton buyers," a complaint endorsed by Assistant Chief Secretary G. F. Sayers, who was inclined "to agree that the Board is rather one-sided. . . ." TNAS 10047/v. III. Secretary of EPCBA to Chief Secretary, January 11, 1932. G. F. Sayers minute on letter, January 12, 1933. This sentiment may not have diminished, even though one of five unofficial seats on an expanded CAB was set aside for a middleman representative of the Eastern Province cotton industry. The TGA retained its two positions, while the cotton industry (Mwanza) had the rest. Then several years later Government struck the Eastern middleman's seat, as noted. Of the four unofficial posts remaining, only two were designated—for the TGA. These two membership revisions affected the official side in minor ways. The first described the Secretary of Native Affairs seat as one for the SNA/Deputy Chief Secretary; the second replaced the SNA/DCS with "a Provincial Commissioner." The Director of Agriculture and Comptroller of Customs always belonged. The unofficial lineup reflected, in short, how the administration estimated the relative lobbying strengths of different groups within the cotton industry.

In that September 1 letter to Scupham, Wakefield criticized the CAB on at least three counts: the unofficials found it "too difficult to be impartial"; the industry had "little confidence" in it; and its recommendations were "too technical." The first count rested on the unrealistic axiom that unofficials should think of the industry as a whole before themselves. The second attests to the fact that the CAB was another guise for government as referee and bound not to please most people some time. The third count partly masked his own ambition, because Wakefield recommended as a solution to excessive technicality that the D/A should grant buying posts on the advice of local authorities. As far as I know, this proposal got nowhere.

41. TNAS 10047/v. III. Secretary, Eastern Province Cotton Buyers Association to Chief Secretary, February 15, 1933.

42. TNAS 25066. Extract from minutes of CAB meeting, March 24, 1937. E. Harrison, invoking clause 38 of Cotton Ordinance No. 12 of 1937, June 10, 1937.

43. African Planters, Kilosa, to Chief Secretary, April 5, 1938.

44. TNAS 26298/I. A. J. Wakefield to Chief Secretary, October 21, 1938. CONFIDENTIAL.

45. TNAS 26298/I. A. J. Wakefield, Notes for Ginners' Meeting Held at Morogoro, November 12, 1938. These are redlined "Personal: not for publication in any form." At that gathering, he analogized a ginnery to a public utility and concluded that "your profits would be assured—they should not be inordinate." He also reminded the ginners that what Government gave it could take away. Their special position will last "only so long as such condition best serves the interests of the cotton industry." While it was unlikely that Government would admit middlemen to areas where none now exist and where volume of cotton does not warrant their entry, he felt ginners should know that a right of occupancy to a ginner for his plot did not mean that government excluded middlemen for the whole ten-year period of the lease.

46. African Planters, Kilosa, to Chief Secretary, March 20, 1939.

47. Acting Chief Secretary to Bwana Saleh bin Yusuf, April 1, 1939.

48. TNAS 22985. A. Sillery minute on January 13, 1936, letter from APA. At that special November 12 meeting with ginners Wakefield asserted that the ring agreement rested on "blackmail." In Morogoro and Kilosa districts "only one store in every cotton market has opened; the rest of the middlemen sit at home idle, yet they get 1 ½ cents/kilo of seed cotton from ginners for output purchased not only at cotton markets but at ginnery

posts and ginneries." Whether ginners were bribing middlemen or middlemen blackmailing ginners is not clear from Wakefield's evidence. He believed this arrangement "merely blackmail, for if they did not pay this levy there would be cut-throat competition."

49. TNAS 25420. Secretary of Middlemen and Cotton Growers Society, Ltd., to Director of Agriculture, July 29, 1937, p. 2. Pledging to introduce an element of competition in cotton buying, this Society, incorporated in Uganda, inquired about purchase licenses and the allotment of cotton stores in the Lake Province. It also complained about the lack of storage space at ginneries. It got nowhere. The Secretariat wasn't sure what kind of facilities the middlemen wanted. And Harrison wrote their Secretary on September 10, 1937, that "this Department does not wish to interfere in any way with the business between cotton buyer and ginner and I would prefer it if you would settle your commercial arrangements without appeal to it." Underneath that statement were control considerations, which could only have been strengthened by a confidential report on the Society from the Ugandan Director of Agriculture. "While I think these people are of little substance," he wrote to Harrison on September 16, 1937, "they will undoubtedly cause trouble and the more cash they can accumulate in Tanganyika, the more likely they will be to cause trouble here. They consist of the middlemen buyer of cotton and some of the 'agitator lawyer type.' They also claim an element of African membership but I have no information on that point."

50. TNAS 25420. Commenting on that letter from the Middlemen and Cotton Growers Society in the Secretariat, G. J. Partridge thought the middlemen "probably right" when they believed the ginners were out "to eliminate them." He conceded that middlemen performed a "useful function," making up part of the "natural forces governing prices [and] the distribution of business." G. J. Partridge minute, September 4, 1937.

51. TNA Lake Province No. 1548 for 1938. D. Sturdy, Memo on Market Improvement and Crop Grading, January 16, 1938.

52. The testimony of Sturdy and others makes it tempting to argue that the Tanganyika administration, by its pricing decisions, may have retarded the growth of cotton output. I shall resist this temptation, because I do not have enough information about the price elasticities of supply for cotton producers from different backgrounds and locations to make a territorial statement.

53. At the ginners' meeting Wakefield recommended an intriguing solution to the "blackmail" he had described, which makes an appropriate sidelight to the price discussion. "Drastic measures" were needed to redirect that 1½ cents/kilo back to the producer. He suggested "zoning the ginneries concerned" and raising ginnery fees to the Uganda level, "which is regarded as safeguarding individual middlemen operating as prime buyers (i.e. those who work for their profit); it does not encourage the entry of large scale middlemen employing paid buyers, and does not place middlemen in a more favourable position than the ginner in the buying of raw cotton." Quoting from a report to agricultural officers, Wakefield asserted that if the Uganda scale were applied, with increased output, the minimum price would rise from one to two cents/kilo. I do not know what evidence from Uganda Wakefield had to buttress his analysis of the varying impact of ginnery fees upon different types of middlemen. Nor did he specify how he would fine-tune existing zoning in the Eastern Province. What I do note here is a recurrence of the notion that price should be a reward: the minimum scale should rise only in response to increased output. I am unable to determine from the files available to me whether Government ever tested Wakefield's "solution" before World War II, but it seems unlikely.

54. TNAS 25066. A. J. Wakefield to Provincial Commissioner, Southern, June 17, 1938.

55. TNAS 21032. Proposal regarding purchase of ginneries of British Cotton Growing Association in the districts of Mwanza, Kwimba, and Biharamulo. P. E. Mitchell to A. A. Willis, Barrister-at-Law, July 25, 1932: "There are, however, strong political and administrative reasons why *Native Administrations* should not engage in commercial ventures, and it has been necessary to turn down propositions, rather on the lines you suggest, which were dependent on the moneys and influence of a Native Administration."

56. Had they achieved a grower-ginner integration, the next step should have included exporting, because there was already considerable vertical integration of ginneries and export firms in Tanganyika.

8.   REGULATING THE COFFEE INDUSTRY: A WARNING FROM THE MOUNTAIN

1. TNAS 11160. H. Wolfe minute, October 24, 1927.

2. Ibid. G. F. Webster to Chief Secretary, July 13, 1928.

3. An uneven and largely futile endeavor to limit the extension of "native" *arabica*-growing took place in the late 1920s and early 1930s. E. A. Brett summarizes most salient details of this attempt in his *Colonialism and Underdevelopment in East Africa: The Politics of Economic Change, 1919-1939* (New York, 1973), pp. 230-31.

4. M. A. Ogutu, "The Cultivation of Coffee among the Chagga of Tanzania, 1919-39," *Agricultural History*, 46 (April 1972):279-90.

5. The shift from ordinary to forked hoe, which the Chagga achieved in the 1920s, may seem minor, along with numerous other inter-war improvements, to those who associate complexity with larger and sometimes more intricate machinery. But the Chagga demonstrated how important well-planned "small" technological adaptations can be for communities that are, in conventional economic terms, capital short. Indeed, those "minor" improvements in the aggregate can pay bigger dividends than great leaps.

6. Two comments eleven years apart by different Directors of Agriculture illustrate the technical level on which much of the European coffee industry in Tanganyika operated. H. Wolfe, in the minute cited in note 1, observed that the "natives'" fields in Kilimanjaro and Meru were cleaner and better cared for than those of the "non-natives." On July 22, 1938, Director A. J. Wakefield, commenting on the depressed state of the European coffee industry, stressed that a "rationalisation" of that enterprise "must come sooner or later" and involve improved plantation methods. In an ironic example, Wakefield noted that "last season there was a move in the right direction when the planters started a Co-operative Society for bulk sales." TNAS 19554, II. A. J. Wakefield to Chief Secretary, July 22, 1938. CONFIDENTIAL.

7. One aim, Dundas wrote, was "to promote coffee growing as a peasant cultivation, each one working his own plot by his own industry with the help of his women and children, so that a class of native employers is not evolved, or at any rate is restricted to a small number comprising only prominent persons." He stated that the formation of cultivators' associations facilitated caring for the *arabica*. CO 691/70. C. C. F. Dundas, Senior Commissioner at Moshi, "Native Coffee Cultivation on Kilimanjaro," May 12, 1924.

8. European growers formed the Kilimanjaro Planters Associaton (KPA), one of several local groups representing "non-native" coffee farmers. In 1930, besides the KPA, there were the Usa, Arusha, and N'Gare Nairobi Planters Associations. These combinations, in turn, made up the Tanganyika Coffee Growers Association, which included more local groups and even the Kilimanjaro Native Co-operative Union. The TCGA was in practice a sometimes petulant European mouthpiece and an often fragmented and ineffective lobby. On any level of organization, most Europeans spent too much time complaining about external factors both imaginary and real—from the largely fabricated dangers of disease posed by proximate "native" plants to the actual subsidies which the German government gave its nationals growing coffee in Tanganyika.

9. *Report of the Marketing Organisation Committee,* Sessional Paper No. 2, January 1931 (Dar es Salaam, 1931), summary.

10. Messrs. Monckton and Company found that the prices they had advanced to growers for several consignments were greater than those they eventually obtained in London during the 1929-30 season. In July 1930, the KNPA faced a shortfall of 24,000 shillings; in August 1930, it still owed the firm 17,000 shillings. The central administration seconded an assistant district officer to assist the Association in financial reorganization; it levied a cess of one kilo per hundredweight bag and wiped out a substantial part of its debt. CO 691/116/30066. "Report on History of KNPA," enclosure no. 3 to CONFIDENTIAL dispatch of May 5, 1931, pp. 9-10.

11. From 1929 on all growers had to join the KNPA and pay it a 2 percent commission. The administration had decided to register all coffee holdings and believed compulsory membership the most effective way to learn the identity of every grower and the size of his enterprise. But producers retained some freedom of action. "In order that the in-

dividual planter, now compelled to become a member of the Association for one particular purpose, should not lose his liberty in other directions," the authors of that KNPA history wrote, "it was specifically laid down in the rules that he should be able to sell his coffee where he pleased [p. 9]." Selling outside the Association required, however, that one still pay it a 2 percent commission on the proceeds.

12. TNAS 26034. Provincial Commissioner G. F. Webster, Northern, to Chief Secretary, February 12, 1932. STRICTLY CONFIDENTIAL. Webster referred to the alleged complicity of Mr. Griffiths, lately auditor of the KNPA, in the purported defalcations of coffee by Molloy and Merinyo and asserted that Mr. Griffiths "does not bear a good reputation," a vague judgment for which I have no corroboration.

13. What heightens a sense of mystery is the fact that Mr. Pennington, who directed the reorganization of the KNPA and should have known the inside story, did not discern the "misappropriations." On April 14, 1931, A. E. Kitching noted, "It is astonishing that these defalcations by Mr. Molloy and officials of the K.N.P.A. should have escaped the notice of Mr. Pennington." TNAS 26034.

14. TNAS 26034. G. F. Webster to Chief Secretary, June 20, 1931. CONFIDENTIAL.

15. Ibid. G. F. Webster cable to Chief Secretary, July 4, 1931.

16. Ibid. G. F. Webster to Chief Secretary, August 25, 1931. CONFIDENTIAL. Governor Stuart Symes varnished the whole procedure in more democratic language for the Colonial Secretary. He asserted that when Merinyo "became aware that an investigation was being made into his conduct and that his arrest was imminent, he endeavoured to obstruct the re-organisation of the Association by disseminating false reports that Government intended to abolish it and to prohibit the growing of coffee by the Chagga tribesmen." Symes described how District Officer Flynn counteracted Merinyo's "subversive movement" and how, "at a large meeting," members of the KNPA "elected Joseph Maliti as President and a new Committee" to replace the one identified with Merinyo. TNAS 13060, II. Governor Stuart Symes to P. Cunliffe-Lister, Secretary of State for Colonies, November 20, 1931. CONFIDENTIAL.

17. TNAS 26034. G. F. Webster to Chief Secretary, August 25, 1931. CONFIDENTIAL.

18. Central administrators never seriously contemplated abolishing the grower organization, but several local officers had stirred up trouble by making their own proposals along those lines. In 1928 Captain Frank C. Hallier, then district officer at Moshi, suggested that the KNPA be abolished and its funds and functions taken over by the Native Authorities. He urged this course "on the grounds that the K.N.P.A. was becoming politically minded and if allowed to develop unchecked would undermine the power and prestige of the Native Authorities." He also proposed to limit the size of the African kihambas (plots). These motions generated a "considerable amount of political ferment," which arrayed the KNPA and Native Authorities against one another. KNPA History, p. 8. Major Dundas, then Secretary of Native Affairs, and the Provincial Commissioner investigated the "ferment" and concluded there was no real hostility between the KNPA and NA. Still, the authors of that 1931 History believed, "The K.N.P.A. had stood for a moment in the role of the champion of the popular rights with the chiefs occupying an ill-defined position in the background [p. 8]." Provincial Commissioner Webster stated that some European planters became involved in the 1928-29 turbulence. Referring to an incident at the end of 1928, he called it a "political upheaval . . . the flames of which were fanned by Mr. Dela Mothe [a Moshi planter] and his followers and developed into nothing more nor less than an attack by Europeans on the Chagga coffee growing industry." TNAS 26034. G. F. Webster to Chief Secretary, August 25, 1931. CONFIDENTIAL.

In October 1929, District Officer Dawkins, Moshi, wrote that the KNPA had outgrown its usefulness to "native" planters as a protective and marketing organization and that an increasing number of growers wanted to sell locally to the highest bidder and evade payment of 2 percent to the KNPA. Secretary of Native Affairs Mitchell sharply criticized Dawkins: "The D.O. is neither helpful nor very intelligent . . . if we have 11,000 unorganised and uncontrolled people to deal with instead of the K.N.P.A. there will certainly be serious consequences." Governor Cameron responded that the Association would continue, for the purposes of registration and disease control, and that Dawkins will try to implement "my wishes." TNAS 11908, I. T. Dawkins to Provincial Commissioner, Northern, October 7, 1929. CONFIDENTIAL. Both Mitchell and Cameron minutes, October 26, 1929.

19. TNAS 13060, II. Marginal note on Strickland's proposals for draft constitution of the KNCU.

20. TNAS 13698. P. E. Mitchell to A. Grieg, Land Officer, July 13, 1932.

21. The need for a general ordinance resulted, in part, from a tortuous examination during 1929 and 1930 which found all then available devices for incorporating the KNPA deficient in some respect. The KNPA could not be registered under Ordinance 7 of 1927 nor under the Companies Act. The Association's nature disqualified it from the purview of Ordinance 7. And "were the Association composed of intelligent people," the Attorney General argued, "to effect their common object it is most likely they would become incorporated under the Companies Act, but I cannot contemplate natives being able to work such a system." He wanted a specific act of incorporation, but Governor Cameron ruled that out, "under existing conditions and in the present state of their development." Secretary Mitchell favored a general ordinance for such associations, and that view prevailed. TNAS 13801. Attorney General minute, September 28, 1929. D. Cameron minute, October 7, 1929. P. E. Mitchell minute, October 6, 1929.

22. CO 691/168. Mr. Lambert's memorandum, March 8, 1939.

23. CO 691/156/42117. D. W. Kennedy to Cecil Bottomley, April 15, 1937. He has distorted the facts here; according to Lambert, ". . . proposals to amend the Co-operative Societies Ordinance were put up but for one reason or another were not proceeded with [in devising the "Chagga Rule"]."

24. Lambert memorandum.

25. Ibid.

26. CO 691/78. "The number of trees to be planted by each planter is now limited to 1000, in order that a native employer class should not be created," wrote the Senior Commissioner, Moshi, on June 30, 1926. This rule was a "dead letter before the end of 1926 and no attempt was made to enforce it," recalled the authors of the KNPA history, although they described its aim less comprehensively: ". . . to ensure that trees would be properly looked after [p. 7]."

27. *Report on the Kilimanjaro Native Co-operative Union,* Sessional Paper No. 4, 1937 (Dar es Salaam, 1937), pp. 25–26.

28. Lambert memorandum.

29. CO 691/159/42254/1. D. W. Kennedy to W. G. A. Ormsby-Gore, September 27, 1937. CONFIDENTIAL.

30. *A Memorandum on the Recent Disturbances in the Moshi District of the Northern Province, Tanganyika Territory,* Sessional Paper No. 1, 1937 (Dar es Salaam, 1937), p. 5.

31. CO 691/159/42254/1. F. Lee minute, November 1, 1937.

32. Lambert memorandum.

33. CO 691/174/42254/1/39. Copy of minute by Solicitor General to Chief Secretary, October 19, 1938.

34. CO 691/168/42254/1. D. W. Kennedy to W. G. A. Ormsby-Gore, April 6, 1938. CONFIDENTIAL.

35. TNAS 25841. Memorandum for Finance Committee on Taxed Legal Costs—Chagga Rule Case, A. L. Pennington for Acting Chief Secretary, July 14, 1938.

36. Local officers tried to put the best face on the outcome. Frank Hallier, then Northern Provincial Commissioner, gave a speech in which he urged the Chagga "to trust the Government. We know what is good for you because we are 1000 years old in experience." The court rulings did not affect the status of the Chagga Council: ". . . when this appeal about the Governor's consent was brought to the East African Court, this Government did not oppose the appeal; it welcomed it because all Chiefs who are recognized by

Government in Tanganyika are the agents of Government, the mouthpieces of Government, but they are not part of the body of Government.'' CO 691/168/42254/1. This file contains a copy of Hallier's speech to the Chagga.

37. TNAS 19938, II. Copy of minutes of first meeting of the Moshi Native Coffee Board, November 23, 1937.

38. Lambert memorandum.

39. CO 691/168/42254/1. H. Cruttwell minute, April 22, 1938.

40. Lambert memorandum.

41. The Tanganyika Governor's deportation power struck the legal firm as ''extraordinary,'' because he could deport people without holding a judicial inquiry. And the accused could not see those ''sworn statements,'' which were secret. In Kenya, by contrast, the Governor was to decide only after a judicial inquiry into the legitimacy of a deportation motion. CO 691/168. Petition by Messrs. Atkinson, Bown, Morrison, and Ainsley to the Secretary of State.

42. CO 691/168. The Tanganyika administration responded to Messrs. Atkinson et al., that ''the wide powers given to the Governor under Cap. 31 [Deportation Ordinance] are, of course, only used in extreme cases.''

43. All the following unnumbered quotations are from the petition. This document is, of course, tendentious. Inferences drawn from activities at meetings in connection with sentences for imprisonment are arguable. Character judgments are especially prone to personal bias, and here there are sharp conflicts between administrators' and petitioners' attitudes. But facts concerning the men's occupations are probably accurate, since petitioners would have little reason to lie about these.

44. Chief Abdiel was more than an antagonist in local disputes over personal matters. In her essay on ''The Chagga'' in *Tradition and Transition in East Africa,* ed. by P. H. Gulliver (Berkeley, 1969), p. 214, Kathleen M. Stahl observed that Chief Abdiel aroused feeling against himself in the 1930s through ''what was thought to be an ambivalent attitude towards the introduction of compulsory co-operative marketing for all Chagga coffee.'' Abdiel first opposed it, then switched and backed the bureaucracy. He was, therefore, identified with the ''Chagga Rule'' and presented a visible personal target for the dissenters. Moreover, he embodied administrative interference in a wider sense. In 1934, Stahl noted, the bureaucracy suggested to the Chagga chiefs that they should have a Paramount Chief. The bureaucracy backed Abdiel; but ''the Chiefs, the only people consulted, clearly favoured Chief Petro Marealle of Marangu, uncle of the future *Mangi Mkuu.*'' The administration then withdrew its suggestion. In any event, Abdiel was a twice-cursed symbol of bureaucratic meddling, in local politics generally and in the KNCU specifically through the ''Chagga Rule.''

45. CO 691/159/52254/2. D. W. Kennedy to W. G. A. Ormsby-Gore, September 27, 1937. CONFIDENTIAL.

46. Provincial Commissioner Hallier wrote that Kiwera was a ''thoroughly bad character and has been evading arrest for more than a year on a charge of undermining the Chief's authority.'' CO 691/168/42254/1. F. C. Hallier to Chief Secretary, March 8, 1938. CONFIDENTIAL.

47. The Tanganyika administration ended up paying the instruction fees and other expenses. Costs awarded against Government totalled 21,825 shillings: a 15,000/– instruction fee and 658/– for other costs in the five original cases; a 5,000/– instruction fee and 1,135/– for other costs in the appeals; and 32/– for taking out decrees. How to slot these disbursements in the budget caused a problem. In the Secretariat J. E. S. Lamb called it ''an unfortunate business . . . I fear the only course is a Special Warrant . . . '' TNAS 25841. J. E. S. Lamb minute, June 18, 1938.

48. All deportees returned home in 1939, except one who had died.

49. CO 691/168/42254/5. G. Bushe minute, March 10, 1939. He also commented on the issue of unauthorized and closed meetings, ''It may be native law, but I feel pretty sure that it would not long remain native law were it not that it is backed by British bayonets.'' Petitioners had also contended, ''The law with regard to the right of assembly seems to be administered in a most peculiar and oppressive fashion by the WaChagga Chiefs with the

support of the Administrative Officers.'' To which assertion the Tanganyika administration replied, ''The idea (not confined to the Chagga) underlying this law is that malcontents should state their grievance in open conclave and before the elders of the tribe. History shows that secret meetings have usually been held for the overthrow of constituted authority. However . . . as Native Administration prospers, a law of this kind may seem out of place. . . .'' But Gov. Mark Young wrote Colonial Secretary MacDonald in 1940 that ''. . . it is advisable to continue to recognize, in the chiefs who now possess it, the power to ban meetings when there is evidence available to show that they are likely to be of such a nature [''seditious conspiracies and unlawful assemblies'']." CO 691/179/42254/5. Mark Young to MacDonald, March 24, 1940.

9. RETROSPECTIVE AND COMPARATIVE AGENDA

1. Readers who want more details on how the Tanganyika administration retarded the emergence of a territorial money market broadly defined should consult "Media as Ends: Money and the Underdevelopment of Tanganyika to 1940," *The Journal of Economic History* 36 (September 1976): 645–62.

2. For further information on how administrators abused some key terms that pertain to economic activity, inspect "Language Manipulation in Colonial Tanganyika, 1919–40," *Journal of African Studies,* 6 (Spring 1979): 9–16.

3. I. Wallerstein, "The Three Stages of African Involvement in the World-Economy," in *The Political Economy of Contemporary Africa,* Peter C. W. Gutkind and Immanuel Wallerstein, eds. (Beverly Hills, 1976), p. 47.

4. E. A. Brett, *Colonialism and Underdevelopment in East Africa: The Politics of Economic Change, 1919–1939* (New York, 1973), p. 305.

5. Ibid., p. 87.

BIBLIOGRAPHY

UNPUBLISHED PRIMARY SOURCES

I have relied extensively on three major collections of unpublished primary material. The first, located in the Public Record Office, London, is the series designated as Colonial Office 691. I studied the contents of all 180 boxes and/or volumes of documentation dealing with the inter-war period. This material includes the correspondence that passed between the Tanganyika administration and Whitehall, sometimes under confidential, secret, or top secret cover, and the numerous minutes and memoranda by various Colonial Office bureaucrats on Tanganyika matters. The second important unpublished primary collection was the set of Secretariat papers preserved in various depositories of the National Archives, Dar es Salaam, Tanzania. The Secretariat files, not all of which are available even to one who has secured the necessary permissions to inspect them, include many written communications among Tanganyika officials from every branch and level of territorial administration, as well as the internal minutes of the Secretariat itself. The third valuable unpublished collection was the Colonial Records Project of Rhodes House Library, Oxford. This project contains, among other things, the private papers and diaries of some leading bureaucrats from inter-war Tanganyika. I found nine sources from three different categories of evidence most illuminating and again thank Rhodes House Library and the men's families for permission to use them.

Diaries (Colonial Records Project Catalogue Numbers)

Gillman, C. MSS. Afr. s. 900(1).
Mitchell, P. E. MSS. Afr. r. 101.

Interview (Colonial Records Project)

J. J. Tawney's interview with D. Sturdy, formerly of Tanganyika's Department of Agriculture, was revealing. The interview was conducted on August 26, 1969.

Papers (Colonial Records Project Catalogue Numbers)

Barnes, W. S. G. MSS. Afr. s. 458–62.
Haarer, Alec Ernest. MSS. Afr. s. 1144.
Hallier, Frank Collings. MSS. Afr. s. 1072.
McGregor, C. J. MSS. Afr. s. 1010.
Page, William Frank. MSS. Afr. s. 274–75.
Wakefield, Arthur John. MSS. Afr. s. 348–53.

PUBLISHED PRIMARY SOURCES

Departmental Reports

The following departments of the Tanganyika bureaucracy issued reports annually during the period, with the stated exceptions:

Agriculture, from 1922.
Audit, from 1928.
Education, from 1923.
Forestry.
Game.
Labour, until 1931.
Land.
Mines. Land and Mines issued joint reports after mid-1930s amalgamation of two departments.
Police.
Public Accounts.
Trade.
Treasury.
Tse-tse Reclamation, from 1929.
Veterinary Science and Animal Husbandry, from 1921.

District and Provincial Books

I read the books preserved on thirty reels of microfilm in Rhodes House Library. These reels are designated as Micr. Afr. 397–399 and 472. Companion works to the Provincial Books were the more widely circulated *Annual Reports of the Provincial Commissioners on Native Administration.*

Sessional Papers (in order of appearance)

Report of the Marketing Organisation Committee. No. 2, 1931.
A Memorandum on the Economics of the Cattle Industry in Tanganyika. No. 1, 1934.
A Memorandum on the Recent Disturbances in the Moshi District of the Northern Province of Tanganyika. No. 1, 1937.
Labour Committee Report for 1936-7. No. 3, 1937.
A Report on the Kilimanjaro Native Co-operative Union. No. 4, 1937.

Special Committee Reports and Administrative Papers

Education of Rural Communities, by R. J. Mason. 1938.
Joint Committee on Closer Union. 1931.
Report of an Education Conference. 1925.
Report of the Central Development Committee. 1940.
Report of the Commission to Inquire into Tanga Disturbances. 1939.
Report of the Committee on Supply and Welfare of Native Labour. 1938.
Report of the East Africa Commission. 1925.
Report of the Labour Inspectorate for 1939. 1940.
Report on Financial Mission to Tanganyika Territory. 1932.
Summary of Proceedings of the Senior Administrative Officers' Conference. 1929.
The Tribes of Tanganyika Territory, Their Districts, Usual Dietary and Pursuits, by R. C. Jerrard. 1936.
Other useful published primary sources were the *Proceedings of the Legislative Council, Tanganyika Territory Reports* to the League of Nations, and the Tanganyika Territory *Gazette.*

UNPUBLISHED SECONDARY SOURCES

Bates, Margaret L. "Tanganyika under British Administration, 1920-1955." Unpublished D. Phil. thesis, Oxford University, 1957.
McCarthy, D. M. P. "The Economic Implications of Indirect Rule in Tanganyika, 1925-39." Unpublished seminar paper presented at Yale University, May 1968.

PUBLISHED SECONDARY SOURCES

Books

Austen, Ralph A. *Northwest Tanzania under German and British Rule.*
New Haven, 1968.

Bennett, N. R. *Mirambo of Tanzania.* New York, 1971.

Brett, E. A. *Colonialism and Underdevelopment in East Africa: The
Politics of Economic Change 1919-1939.* New York, 1973.

Duignan, Peter, and Gann, L. H., eds. *Colonialism in Africa,
1870-1960.* 5 vols. London, 1969-1975.

Gifford, P., and Louis, W. R., eds. *Britain and Germany in Africa.* New
Haven, 1967.

Gulliver, P. H., ed. *Tradition and Transition in East Africa.* Berkeley,
1969.

Gutkind, Peter C. W., and Wallerstein, Immanuel, eds. *The Political
Economy of Contemporary Africa.* Beverly Hills, 1976.

Harlow, Vincent, and Chilver, E. M., eds. *History of East Africa.* Vol. 2.
Oxford, 1965.

Heussler, R. *Yesterday's Rulers.* Syracuse, 1963.

Hill, Polly. *Studies in Rural Capitalism in West Africa.* Cambridge,
1970.

Iliffe, John. *Tanganyika under German Rule.* Cambridge, 1969.

Jacoby, Henry. *The Bureaucratization of the World.* Berkeley, 1973.

Kay, Geoffrey B. *The Political Economy of Colonialism in Ghana: A Collection of Documents and Statistics, 1900-1960.* Cambridge, 1972.

———. *Development and Underdevelopment: A Marxist Analysis.* New
York, 1975.

Leubuscher, Charlotte. *Tanganyika Territory: A Study of Economic
Policy under Mandate.* London, 1944.

Low, D. A., and Smith, Alison, eds. *History of East Africa.* Vol. 3. Oxford, 1976.

MacGuire, C. Andrew. *Towards 'Uhuru' in Tanzania: The Politics of
Participation.* Cambridge, 1969.

McPhee, A. *The Economic Revolution in British West Africa.* London,
1926.

Oliver, R., and Mathew, G., eds. *History of East Africa.* Vol. 1. Oxford,
1963.

Ruthenberg, Hans. *Agricultural Development in Tanganyika.* Berlin,
1964.

Shanin, Teodor, ed. *Peasants and Peasant Societies*. Middlesex, England, 1971.

Shivji, Issa. *Class Struggles in Tanzania*. New York, 1976.

Journals

"Official Documents." *American Journal of International Law Supplement*, 13 (1919), pp. 137–38.

"Official Documents." *Supplement to the American Journal of International Law*, 18 (July 1923), pp. 153–57.

Ogutu, M. A. "The Cultivation of Coffee among the Chagga of Tanzania, 1919–39." *Agricultural History*, 46, no. 2 (April 1972), pp. 279–90.

INDEX

Abdiel, Chief. *See* Shangali, Chief Hery Abdiel
Administrators' Conference (Dar es Salaam), 52
African Planters Association (APA): protest and implications, 82–90, 92, 130 n. 38
Agriculture: manipulation of. *See* "Plant-More-Crops" Campaign
Amari, Saleke, 82
Amery, L., 25
Ananduni, Anderson, 107
Arab Association, 59–60
Armitage-Smith, Sir Sydney, 21–22, 119 n. 22
Arusha Planters Association, 133 n. 8
Arusha (town), 21, 106–7

Bagshawe, F. J., 123 n. 50
Bahi township, 57
Baker, E. C., 16–17
Bankruptcy Bill, 40
Baraka, Kombo, 120 n. 24
Barnes, W. S. G., 56, 62
Biharamulo district, 132 n. 55
bin Imangi, Issa, 48
bin Mafalu, Toma, 106–7
bin Matinga, Ndaskoi, 104
bin Mbatia, William, 104
bin Selemani, Abdullah, 82
Boyd-Moss, Hon. Brig., 28, 40
Brett, E. A., 113, 119 n. 17, 119 n. 19, 133 n. 3
Brett, F. W., 61
British Cotton Growing Association, 92
British mandate for East Africa: 37; Article 3, 5; Article 6, 38; Article 7, 31; Donald Cameron's interpretation of Article 3, 5–6
British Treasury. *See* Treasury (British)
Budgets: limitations on information contained therein, 11–12
Bukoba African Association, 47
Bukoba district, 61
Bukoba incident (1928–1929), 70

Bukoba (town), 33, 46, 61
Bulk marketing, 34, 97
Bureaucracy: calculus of maximization and minimization, 10, 21, 64; chain of command as unifying agency, 7; exhibits ethos of British overseas colonial service, 4–5; as signficant force in its own way, 5; table of organization, 6–7. *See also* Bureaucratic economy; Indirect rule (Administration); Native Administration (Authorities); Secretariat
Bureaucratic economy: axioms, 9; calculus, 10, 21, 64; definition of, 5; framework of extraction and control the core of, 10; official market organization, 50–51, 62–63; "Plant-More-Crops" Campaign, 64; Summary of harmful consequences, 110–12, 113
Bushe, G., 109, 136 n. 49
Byatt, Horace, 74, 115
Byrne, Bishop, 105

Callander, C. A., 81
Cameron, Donald, 5–7, 25, 40, 42, 51, 65, 81, 115, 118 n. 7 (Chap. 1), 126 n. 23, 129 n. 5, 129 n. 7, 135 n. 18, 135 n. 21
Campbell, D. C., 53, 85, 87
Central Development Committee, 21
Central Province, 52–53, 57–59, 64, 74–75, 118 n. 9
"Chagga Rule": legal proceedings and related matters, 100–105, 107–8, 135 n. 23, 135 n. 36, 136 n. 44, 136 n. 47; origins, 97–98; voluntariness of Kilimanjaro Native Co-operative Union negated, 99
Chagga (WaChagga) (society): 4, 46, 74, 93–97, 100–106, 108–9, 134 n. 16, 134 n. 18, 135 n. 36, 136 n. 44, 136 n. 49; coffee growers differentiated, 101; coffee-growing industry, 94; significance of protest, 108–9; technological change, 133 n. 5

145

DENNIS M. P. McCARTHY is associate professor of history, Iowa State University. He holds master's and doctoral degrees from Yale University and was associate member, St. Antony's College, Oxford, in 1970 and 1971. Besides this book he has written articles for the professional journals of his fields, including the *International Journal of African Historical Studies* and the *Journal of Economic History*. His research interests encompass the historical evolution of meanings and patterns of underdevelopment, and, at present, an investigation of comparative African colonial bureaucracies.